I

HATE

FUN

I
HATE
FUN

by
Mifflin Lowe

PRICE STERN SLOAN
Los Angeles

Dedicated to Mimi and Dabby. Without your inspiring examples, I wouldn't have this foul sense of humor.

Illustrations and front cover photo hand-tinting by Rick Penn-Kraus

© 1991 by Mifflin Lowe
Illustrations © 1991 by Price Stern Sloan, Inc.
Front cover photo © 1991 by Gene Dwiggins
Back cover photo © 1991 by Anthony Nex

Published by Price Stern Sloan, Inc.
11150 Olympic Boulevard
Suite #650
Los Angeles, California 90064

Printed in U.S.A.
9 8 7 6 5 4 3 2 1

Lowe, Mifflin.
    I hate fun/Mifflin Lowe.
        p.   cm.
    ISBN 0-8431-2885-2
    I.   Title.
    PN6162.L588   1991
    818' .5402--dc20   90-23578
                                            CIP

This book has been printed on acid-free paper.

Table of Contents

THE "F" WORD: AN AUTHOR'S INTRODUCTION

"Much of Man's misery may be attributed to a simple inability to remain happily alone in a room by himself."

René Descartes

We are a people desperate to have fun. Look in any direction and you can see hundreds of us joylessly driving off to resorts in overloaded station wagons, boarding jet planes with pathetically overpacked suit cases and frantically hailing crosstown taxis in search of a trendier restaurant or a hotter nightspot. The obvious problem is that when we get to these places, we invariably notice that the only people smiling are those collecting admission. The rest of us look worried, irritated or bored. Typically, we return from a fun spot wishing we'd just stayed home. Memory is short, however, and the fun mongers amongst us are relentless. Soon, we fall prey to the blandishments of someone who promises us a good time; and the insidious cycle repeats itself. We go to Disneyland, a new restaurant and New Hampshire. All in all, we've been so brainwashed we no longer stop to wonder whether the fun we're pursuing is something we enjoy!

Well, I say it's time to end the tyranny! It's time to expose fun for the fraud it is. I dedicate this book to everyone who's ever been forced to dance the hula, chug a can of beer, or go to a New Year's Eve party. The next time you're approached by some irrepressible, insufferable lover of fun, I hope these pages will give you the simple courage to stand up and reply, "I HATE FUN."

Mifflin Lowe

1

Young Fun:
It's Enough to Make You Primal Scream

TOYS

"There is no absurdity so palpable but that it may be firmly planted in the human head if you only begin to inculcate it before the age of five, by constantly repeating it with an air of great solemnity."

Arthur Schopenhauer

As a child, you will be exposed to the word "fun" more than at any other time in your life—mostly on TV commercials. They will, for instance, tell you it's fun to eat cereal right out of the box. What on earth could they be talking about? Eating cereal right out of the box is much like eating shrapnel. Unsoftened by milk, cereal is dry, brittle and can make your gums bleed. Worse yet you will not even have the solace of being able to mash the brutal nuggets around your milky bowl with a Mickey Mouse spoon. You must merely chew, grimace and swallow, not without great difficulty, each pasty mouthful. Frequently you see cereal boxes also promise–in florescent letters, half as high as the box itself–you'll find a fun toy inside. Invariably you'll find the fun toy is nothing more than a shapeless blob of plastic with no discernable function. Typically this will lead you to the conclusion, perhaps for the first time in your life, that you've been swindled.

While this may be your first taste of disappointment, it will hardly be your last. As life proceeds, you will learn much about fun and fraud and toys. You will learn that toy guns don't shoot real bullets, talking dolls never say anything new, sea monkeys aren't really monkeys, ant farms aren't farms, bubbles always burst and boys' bicycles are designed to castrate them at an early age. (Seriously, why do boys' bikes have the bar across the middle, while girls' bikes don't?) In general you will learn that

4

anything put together falls apart, everything looks great on TV but nothing works at home and nothing ever lasts, especially if your father has to assemble it. As the years roll by, you will find with ever mounting dismay that not once will a toy be half as much fun as an advertiser has promised. Thus by the tender age of seven you will have a deep appreciation of one of life's important lessons: fun is a word people mainly use when they're trying to sell you something!

THE PLAYGROUND

Kids are curious and like to learn from each other. Sadly, they like to learn from each other much the same way scientists like to learn from laboratory rats, that is by performing experiments that barely take into consideration the fact that the subject is a living, sentient being. Typically, these are the things kids are curious about:

- **How high do they have to push a swing before you fall off?**

- **What will happen if they get off a seesaw at the bottom, while you're at the top?**

- **What will happen if they shove a stick into the spokes of your bicycle while you're riding it?**

- **How will you react if they throw you a string of firecrackers?**

- **If you're bound, gagged and pushed off the top of a sliding board, what are the chances you'll survive?**

In short, until kids reach an age at which they've been properly socialized, they're indisputably vicious and must be treated as though insane. As their playmate, you are nothing more than fodder for their savage imaginations. If you're a girl, the playground is the place you're most likely to have somebody look up your dress without even asking first. If you're a boy, you'll find your confreres will have few compunctions about popping you in the mouth with a baseball bat, poking you in the eye with a stick and generally engaging in other activities that are not considered amusing anywhere outside a Three Stooges fan club.

Furthermore, when you're not being tormented on a playground, you may expect to be bored. After all, just what the hell are you supposed to do on one of those cement turtles? Should you sit on it? Jump on it? Or is it just there to chip your teeth? And what about those inexplicable, ubiquitous automobile tires? What are you supposed to do with them? Kick them? Chew on them? Besides, if all those tires weren't in playgrounds, they'd probably be in toxic waste dumps. Are they really something for kids to play with?

THE CIRCUS

By the time you're three or four years old, you've already opened a box of cereal and discovered that the promised, much-ballyhooed toy inside is nothing more than a useless, formless blob of plastic. In short, you have already tasted disappointment but do not yet know despair. But there is still a ray of hope glimmering in the long tunnel of years which stretches out before you: the circus.

"Lions, tigers, elephants! Fun!" your father will shout. "Bears on bicycles, trapeze artists, clowns! Fun!" your mother will shriek. You will, of course, be skeptical. You will sense from the desperation of your parents' enthusiasm that you are, once again, doomed to disillusionment. Nonetheless, you will be optimistic. Maybe the clowns will be amusing. Maybe the elephants will be incredible. After all, who wants to be a four-year-old Soren Kierkegaard?

Finally the big day will arrive. At the circus grounds you will be surrounded by families such as your own—two hopeful adults leading a perplexed child toward a distant tent. At some point, you will come upon a large clump of compacted mud and hay. "What's that?" you will inquire innocently. "Elephants." your father will snicker. "Elephants?" you will think. All along you'd thought elephants were huge animals, not big clumps of clay and hay. "Pooh pooh," your father will explain.

A vein will throb in your head. You've come expecting glitter, glamour, the greatest show on earth. The first thing you've seen is the greatest dung heap imaginable. Already things are not going right. The grin of expectation will begin a long, slow slide from your face. You will stumble toward the Big Top in a stupor. Once inside, you will be choked by a new and undefinable smell. It will be the rare combination of elephant excrement, clowns and cotton candy. Your parents will ask if you want something to eat. You would, of course, love something to eat, if only the odor didn't make you want to retch. When you decline, your parents will look at each other quizzically. Shortly after you take your seat, the master of ceremonies will appear in the center ring. Without knowing what a pimp is, you will instinctively know he looks like one. When he starts the Parade of Performers, introducing each with a spiel that is both hyperbolic and insincere, it will disturb you that such an obvious phoney is not only permitted to appear in public, but is actually in charge of things. This is something you will have cause to reconsider every four years throughout your life during presidential elections.

The Parade of Performers itself will remind you of a Hieronymous Bosch painting. The elephants, those prodigious producers of pooh, will be foolishly festooned in cheap ornaments and gaudy headpieces, and will be ridden by women who are similarly dressed. They will be followed by dogs in dresses lurching on their hind legs, bears on bicycles wearing hats, dwarves, midgets and clowns. In their uniform perversion of nature, they will make you want to cry. Even the clowns, both pathetic and irritating in their efforts to elicit applause, will be tired, old men with wrinkles so deep not even gobs of makeup can conceal them. They will remind you of janitors in drag. You will cling to the hope that, somehow heroic, the trapeze artists will redeem this tasteless display. When a troupe of pudgy people clad in tired tights appears, you will slump in your seat. The wild animals are now your only hope. Perhaps some long suppressed instinct will reassert itself! Perhaps they will maul a midget, turn on their trainer or claw a clown! But, alas, no. In meek obedience, they will jump through hoops, walk in circles and sit placidly on painted boxes, responding to every cracked whip and shouted command.

When you get home, your parents will teasingly ask if you want to run away and join the circus. You will want to tell them only the sad victims of incest and child abuse could consider this an improvement of their fates. Years before you hear the word "tawdry," you will have a profound understanding of what it means. It is the circus.

LITTLE LEAGUE SPORTS

Left to their own devices, kids generally know how to have a good time. Given a choice, a child will, for instance, make a mudpie, throw a stick or engage in some other form of harmless nonsense, playing what he wants and quitting when he wishes. At some point, however, this is simply not good enough for some parents, many of whom seem to feel the same way about kids that Jimmy Hoffa used to feel about workers: they can't possibly be happy unless they're organized. This means Little League. This means uniforms.

As soon as you see a kid in a uniform, you may assume that the good times are over—at least for the kid. Inevitably, the child will be forced to chose between being a dwarfish parody of a professional athlete or a humbled outcast. You see, no matter what the sport, the Little League experience is always the same. If you stink, you will be yelled at by the coach, booed by friends and scorned by neighbors. Thus, by age twelve, you will be left with a crushed and broken spirit. On the other hand, if you're good, you will be forced to play incessantly, even when injured, by a coach who considers himself a reincarnation of Vince Lombardi. Thus, by age twelve, you will be left with a crushed and broken body. In either case, by the time the grown-ups are done meddling, playing a Little League sport will be about as much fun as belonging to the Hitler Youth movement. Besides, before you decide to become a little jock, shouldn't you seriously consider why you're supposed to wear one?

LITTLE LEAGUE BASEBALL

If the coach puts you in right field, this means you really stink. This means that if a ball is ever hit to you, it will either a) hit you on the bridge of the nose or b) go between your legs and roll all the way to the wall for a home run. If you're good, on the other hand, the coach will make you a pitcher. This means you'll be forced to throw beanballs at erstwhile friends, and stand in the perfect position to get hit by vicious line drives. This is fun?

LITTLE LEAGUE FOOTBALL

If you're pudgy and slow, your coach will make you a lineman. This means you'll get knocked down a lot, have your nose ground in the dirt, and nobody will ever know your name. Anyway, the grappling you engage in, with your counterpart on the other team, will look like nothing more than a belly-bucking contest between belligerent baby Buddahs. On the other hand, if you're fast and shifty, your coach will put you in the backfield. This means the entire opposing team will spend a lot of time and effort trying to give you a permanent spinal injury. Either way you will soon walk with a limp. Some choice.

LITTLE LEAGUE BASKETBALL

Little League basketball makes about as much sense as Little League cross-dressing. The ball is bigger than most of the participants, and the basket is far enough above their heads that they can barely see it. Consequently, a game typically turns into little more than a gang of squirming squirts writhing in the vicinity of an orange rubber sphere. In short, before a certain age, basketball is not really a sport at all, but merely a pig pile with referees.

SUMMER CAMP

All during the winter, your parents will try to persuade you to go to summer camp. They will use the "f" word with astonishing frequency. What kind of fun are they talking about? They are talking about building birdhouses and making wallets. In short, menial labor. They are talking also about hiking, during which you might get bitten by a poison toad, and water polo during which you could drown. In short, life-threatening activities. Now, just why do you suppose they're doing this? Do you really think they're willing to spend two thousand dollars a week so you can make a birdhouse not even a starling would live in or make a wallet that you could get for less than twenty-five cents at any yard sale? No, my fond young one. Clearly the reason your parents want you to go to summer camp is so they can go someplace else without you. You see, while summer camps are supposed to be places that let kids spend a few weeks every summer with their friends, they actually exist so that parents can spend a few weeks every summer without their kids.

The truth is summer camps are nothing more than high-rent internment camps with vaguely Indian names. Just as in any internment camp, the fundamental issue is survival. Rule number one is to look out for number one. The other campers are simply not your friends. They will be only too happy to leave you up a creek without a paddle, throw flaming marshmallows down your shirt, give you a humiliating nickname and generally do lots of other stuff you can read about in *Lord of the Flies*.

Sadly rule number two is that the camp counselors aren't your friends either. In fact, camp counselors are underpaid young people whose interest lies exclusively in trying to get into each other's pants and not just for a three-legged race. To a camp counselor, you see, a moment not spent actively trying to compromise the virtue of another counselor is, without question, a moment wasted. Keep this in mind when you're out in water over your head or doing anything else that could endanger your life. The simple truth is that you'll have to look out for your own butt, because a camp counselor will probably be looking at someone else's. Remember that unlike the President, members of Congress and Supreme Court Justices, camp counselors don't have to answer to anybody and there's no system of checks and balances to keep them in line. When it comes to you, a camp counselor has absolute authority, so don't start whining and complaining. If you do, your counselor will simply assign the bunk above yours to a chronic bed wetter. It can make for a long summer.

BOARD GAMES

Following several days of bad weather, an implacable restlessness sprouts in the souls of children—a nameless, formless discontent that grows with the festering urgency of a single-celled slime mold. Soon in living rooms throughout the land, children are whining, moping and getting in their parents hair. Inevitably, a board game is produced. Boards are laid open on the living room rug and pursued according to the time-honored formula: I came; I argued bitterly; I went home in a huff.

THE UNIVERSAL RULES OF PLAY

First there'll be an argument about which game to play. Once it's determined which game to play, there'll be an argument concerning who goes first. Ultimately, the player who goes first will be either (a) the one in whose house the game is played, or (b) whoever decides to roll the dice before anyone else, or possibly (c) the biggest.

Once it has been decided who goes first, there'll be an argument about the rules of the game. After a thorough review of the rule book, everyone will agree that the rules don't make any sense and that no one understands them. Ultimately, it will be decided to play the game the way it was played last time, which no one remembers anyway.

Once play begins anyone who starts to win may immediately gloat and make fun of either all other players or any single player of his choice. Once it becomes apparent to any player that he can't possibly win, that player is empowered to throw the dice under the couch, flip over the board or kick all playing pieces under the refrigerator or any other large household appliance.

At this point, whoever is ahead will claim that the game is over and that he won. In the event it cannot be clearly determined who was ahead, any player may claim he was going to win on his next move. Conversely, any player who was clearly not in a position to win may now claim that nobody won since the game was never played to conclusion. In either case, all players will argue loudly, illogically and violently about who won or didn't win, the degree of each player's stupidity and perhaps the status of each one's legitimacy.

At this point, the mother of the child in whose house the game is being played will tell all players to be quiet or go home. After a hiatus of about two days, during which all players will refuse to talk to each other, play will resume at the house of any mother other than the mother of the child at whose house the original game was played.

MUSIC LESSONS

For most people, the attempt to play music is nothing more than an advanced form of embarrassment. There are a few specialists in the world—"freaks" they would be called in other contexts—who can actually play instruments well enough that someone else would want to listen to them. For everyone else, however, playing music is nothing more than a painful and prolonged form of humiliation. If you play the guitar, you will get your fingers stuck between the strings. If you play the piano, you will always hit at least one wrong note. If you play the violin or the saxophone, you will be exposed to an excruciating screech within mere inches of your ear. And, if you play the clarinet, you will be accused of harboring perverse, though repressed, sexual desires.

For some reason, however, parents frequently encourage kids to take music lessons. This is clearly not because they expect to enjoy hearing their children play musical instruments. Just as every kid instinctively knows that taking music lessons will be as enjoyable as finishing his peas, so does every parent know that listening to a child play a musical instrumen, will be akin to having the temporal lobe split with an ice pick. Unaccountably, many parents, once a week, continue to shove their kids in the direction of a music teacher with the promise that playing an instrument will be something the child will enjoy later in life. Parents tell children this because playing music is something kids clearly don't enjoy as children; and it is only with this distant promise that parents can get kids to stop cavorting with childhood chums and relegate a sunny afternoon to the tedium of practicing scales.

Of course, none of this makes sense. First of all, everyone hates listening to kids play music as much as a kids hate playing it. Second, just think about it. Will you really enjoy playing music when you get older? As you age, do you imagine your increasingly arthritic fingers will even be able to perform the complex calisthenics required to play? Do you suppose your increasingly opaque eyes will be able to make sense of the marching army of ants which constitutes a written page of music? And no matter how old you get, do you suppose you'll ever truly rid yourself of the gnawing inner terror, telling you that at any moment you could hit a preposterous and humiliating clinker—a note so foul that anyone within earshot will turn, wince and snicker?

This is fun? No way, José. The fact is, not only does music deprive you of the chance to cavort with your childhood chums, it will simply never be fun. No matter how old you get, any time you sit down to play, you're much more likely to wind up with Hungarian goulash than Hungarian rhapsody. Besides, how does it make you feel to know that Mozart was composing music, at the age of three, that you'll never be able to play in your life?

PETS

When you are young, you will torment your parents to buy you a pet. This is because you know nothing about animals. To persuade your parents to let you have one, you will promise to love and cherish your pet. You will promise to wash and feed it. You will promise to feed it and walk it everyday. The next time you will make so many extravagant promises, with absolutely no intention of keeping them, will be during your wedding ceremony.

At any rate, within two weeks of getting a pet, you will be utterly bored with it. Nonetheless, your parents will insist that you continue to feed it, bath it and, most grotesquely, clean up after it. In short, the little critter you fell in love with no longer will be the same charming creature you saw in the pet store. It will be a burden. You see, the fundamental question when you get a pet is not who's going to take care of it, but who owns whom? What's more, inevitably your pet will reproduce and your problems will multiply. So please, remember, no matter how cute and cuddly it may look in a pet shop window, a pet by any other name is still just an animal.

THE KITTY NITTY GRITTY

One day you will go to the SPCA and get an irresistible kitten. Within a few months, it will no longer be a little kitty. It'll be a big, fat cat. Soon your house will smell like a litter box. Your furniture will be torn to shreds. Your forearms and ankles will look like steak tartare. If your cat sleeps with you, it will demand half the bed. Every morning, it will wake you up by pouncing on (a) your face or (b) your genital area. This is because he wants you to get up and put food in his bowl. This does not mean he wants to eat, however. At least, not what you're serving.

DOGS

Just as the great white shark is nature's perfect eating machine, the dog is nature's perfect excreting machine. This means that even on bitter winter nights someone will have to take your dog outside for a walk, and will have to clean up after it. This someone is you.

HAMSTERS, GERBILS AND WHITE MICE

These putative pets have the uncanny ability to instantly give, even the most magnificent residence, the ambience of a pet shop. They kick wood shavings onto the floor. They eat and eliminate incessantly. Ultimately, they make an entire house smell like a pet shop. Is this where you want to invite guests and entertain friends? Someplace that smells like a pet shop? What's more, these creatures simply have nothing that could be expected to endear them to humans. No personality. No nifty little tricks. They're not even particularly interesting at which to look. They're just there, running with a sort of rodential rage on those asinine treadmills. Some rodents even eat their own newborn. No wonder they're used in laboratory experiments. Who could care if they're dead or alive? If it weren't for their treadmills, who would know?

EASTER CHICKS AND BABY DUCKS

In most American homes, these pets have an average life span of exactly one day. Typically you will come downstairs the morning after acquiring one of these creatures, hoping to kiss, hug and feed it, only to find that it went to birdie heaven during the night. What's the point?

16

SNAKES, TURTLES, FISH AND ALLIGATORS

They live in muck and mire. They crawl through slime. They eat flies and worms and are entirely devoid of personality. In short, they're a lot like insurance salesmen. Is this what you want for a pet?

RECESS

Recess, of course, is supposed to be fun. The problem is that, if you're a boy, recess is the time you're most likely to get beaten up and have your lunch money stolen. If you're a girl, recess is when someone is most likely to look up your dress without asking first. What's more, even if neither of these two things happens, recess is when you'll have to play games like dodgeball, during which classmates will try to hit you in the face with a rubber ball that is three times the size of your head.

Later in high school, of course, recess won't be called recess anymore. It will be called gym class. During gym class, you will frequently find yourself pitted against brutal youths who should really be playing some sort of professional contact sport instead of occupying valuable classroom space. Playing with them will not be systematic exercise so much as an exercise in systematic humiliation. To avoid this daily ritual of abuse, you will have to bring a note from your mom claiming that you're sick or a letter from your doctor explaining that you have a heart murmur. This way you probably won't get beaten up during gym class. You'll get beaten up later in the locker room.

AMUSEMENT PARKS

Any place with something called a fun house is predictably loathsome. Ironically, an amusement park is one place you may never expect to be amused. Nauseated? Yes. Revolted? Perhaps. Scared witless? Of course. But amused? Hardly. Most rides at an amusement park will make you want to throw up. The others will be boring. This is fun?

Something else you should consider at an amusement park is that the geeks aren't just in the show, they run the show. Seriously, the few ride operators who don't look like the pathetic products of centuries of inbreeding tend to resemble members of the Manson gang. So why are you putting your life in their hands?

Of course, it's your life, so you can do what you want with it, but just suppose you die on one of those preposterous rides. Inevitably, during your last seconds on earth it will occur to you that everyone at your funeral will know you died on something called a "Salt and Pepper Shaker." Do you expect them not to laugh? This is not what's called "death with dignity." Even if you live, here's the sort of amusement you can expect at an amusement park.

- If you're afraid to stand up on a roller coaster, your friends will call you a chicken.

- If you're not afraid to stand up on the roller coaster, you'll be decapitated.

- You will ride on a rickety, old Ferris wheel that hasn't been inspected since it was built, and become stranded at the top. You will swing freely back and forth in the breeze, being able to contemplate precisely where your body will hit the ground.

- You will see a sideshow with two-headed sheep, chickens with hair, tattooed women, dwarves, pinheads, fat ladies, Siamese twins, hermaphrodites, bearded women and lots of other stuff you could see just by walking down Upper Broadway.

• If you go on a "kiddie ride" you will not get to steer. Whether the ride is ostensibly a boat, car or train, it will just go around in circles until the fat guy in the sweaty undershirt who runs the thing decides it's time for you to get off.

• Within half an hour of arrival, your hair, face and hands will be covered with a fine glaze of cotton candy while the rest of you will be tacky from the sticky stuff they put on candy apples. You will never feel truly clean again.

• You will engage in tests of strength and skill at which you will fail miserably. Pimple-faced boobs will openly laugh at you. A carnival barker with a lesser brain than that possessed by a brontosaurus will dismiss you with contempt. You will experience a sense of profound shame and humiliation. Is this the sort of fun you were looking for?

Adolescent Behavior

NO WONDER THEY CALL IT ADOLESCENCE

During your teen years, the "f" word will be used to describe an astonishing array of activities and experiences as well as sell you almost everything from clothes and cocaine to soda pop. Clearly at this time of life, the concept of fun means different things to different people. To your peers, fun generally means doing almost anything that could get you thrown out of the house, kicked out of school or put in jail; for instance, stealing a car, flushing light bulbs down the boys' room toilets or mooning the vice-principal. To your parents, on the other hand, fun is anything that will keep you out of the house but under the surveillance of adults. Typically this means they'd like you to belong to a church group, which is something normal adolescents consider only somewhat less embarrassing than having a large, purple zit in an obvious place.

At any rate, as a teenager, you must be cautioned to remember that it wasn't so long ago that you still believed in Santa Claus and the Easter Bunny and that you're still pretty likely to believe just about anything anybody tells you. You should also remember that, as an adolescent, you will be subject to a force which, in the entire universe, may be second in strength only to that exerted by a black hole. I refer, of course, to the brutal, benthic power of our teen culture's infamous "peer pressure." This pressure will be exerted at critical junctures throughout your adolescence in order to get you to try a lot of things for the very first time which, in all probability, you had no intention of trying at all. At any rate, be careful. A lot of your peers will consider it the highest form of amusement to endanger your health and sanity by, for instance, convincing you to dive headfirst into a murky, quarry pool or ride a motorcycle blindfolded with somebody on your shoulders.

It's probably also worth mentioning that, during adolescence, the word "fun" will frequently be used in conjunction with the word "chicken." For instance, someone trying to encourage you to indulge in an impromptu session of bungee jumping may well try to clinch his case by saying something such as "Come on, it'll be fun. What are you....chicken?" The truth, of course, is that you are, indeed, "chicken." If you weren't afraid to jump off a bridge with a rope tied to your ankles, you'd have to be considered insane.

In all probability, it's due to the insatiable adolescent appetite for fun that accidents always have been the leading cause of death among teens. Suicide is second. I'm not sure what the connection is, but it might have something to do with the fact that it's the only way you can get your peers to leave you alone. Somehow though, you'll probably manage to get through adolescence alive and, sooner or later, you'll figure out that no such thing as fun exists and that you can simply go about the business of leading a dull, ordinary life just as God intended. Until then, here's some more of the fun you can expect to have.

FIRST SMOKE

Smoking your first cigarette is one of those experiences which strongly intimates that becoming an adult may not be as much fun as you'd hoped. You will choke, you will cough, your lungs will ache and your eyes will burn, while tears dribble from them, as you gasp desperately for air. The only other form of fun that's clearly comparable is being smothered with a moldy throw rug. Nevertheless, smoking is a grown-up thing to do, so you can more or less count on the fact that sooner or later you will get your hands on a cigarette, set it on fire and stick it in your mouth.

Since the experience is unarguably unpleasant and painful, the question arises: Why do adolescents do it? The answer, of course, is that many adolescents think it makes them look more adult. The question then arises: Why would adolescents want to look like adults, a class of humans that they unapologetically hate? Good question.

FIRST DRINK

Calling this your "first drink" is, of course, a euphemism for the more accurate and proper title which should be your "first drunk." You see, as an adolescent who's accustomed to ripping open the fridge and gulping down about a quart and a half of soda pop or milk directly from the bottle without pausing for a breath, you're simply not accustomed to moderation when it's time to imbibe.

This is something that will become entirely clear to you when you're approximately halfway through the bottle of Old Grandad you've either stolen from your parents or paid some unfortunate wino to buy for you. At this point a rising sense of nausea and a swirling sense of vertigo may give you a brief intuition that you should stop. You will, however, continue to guzzle the Old Grandad as though it were mother's milk. This is because you will be surrounded by friends and acquaintances who will stand around to make sure you drink the whole bottle without missing a drop, just the way your mom used to stand around to make sure you swallowed all your medicine without spitting any out. The operative principal here is simply this: Your first taste of alcohol will make you want to puke. If it doesn't your friends will make sure you keep drinking until it does.

FIRST TIME BEHIND THE WHEEL

The first time you drive a car will be an unforgettable experience for at least one person. Usually, it will be the person teaching you. Incredibly the act of driving, an act so undemanding that we permit those who are nearly blind and virtually dead to perform it on our public highways, suddenly becomes, to even the most alert and athletic teenager, something akin in complexity to the vast coordination of events required for "Operation Desert Shield."

You will step on the gas and the car will lurch. You will jam on the brakes and the wheels will screech. You will shift gears and forget the clutch. CRUNCH, OOPS! You will turn without signalling and signal without turning. You will venture forth, tentatively, onto the highway. OH MY GOD! LOOK OUT! OOPS! SORRY, I DIDN'T SEE THAT ONE. Merging, that simple, seemless task your mother performs every day, will seem like an impossibility. Imminent death will appear as the only probability. Cars will pass, honking. Drivers will pass, screaming and making rude hand gestures. Next to you in the car, the person who has calmly agreed to teach you how to drive will be (a) joining the other drivers in screaming and making rude hand gestures expressive at you, or (b) entering a state of catatonia. SORRY. DID YOU PASS OUT OR WHAT? OOPS, SORRY, I DIDN'T SEE THAT ONE EITHER.

FIRST PARTY

The main thing you should know about your first party is that even though it will be given at your house, you will have very little to say about when it takes place or who will come. These matters will be determined by your peers. When your parents are away for the weekend, in the hospital, vacationing in Europe or otherwise unavailable for immediate comment, a few acquaintances will simply decide it's time for your first party and start showing up. In that regard, another thing to keep in mind about your first party is that you will have nothing to say about the guest list. As mentioned, the first guests will be a few friends. These will be followed by friends of your friends, followed by friends of your friends' friends, followed by friends you haven't seen in years as well as friends you didn't know you had, and before you know it, everyone will be dancing on the tables, enjoying your parents liquor and playing catch with your mom's crystal. Eventually, of course, the cops will also come. That's how you'll know the party's over.

FIRST DATE

During adolescence you will undergo new and confusing experiences, such as growing breasts and sprouting pubic hair. Why these things should confuse anybody is beyond me, but all the authorities agree that these things do, so I suppose they must. At any rate, once you either grow breasts or sprout pubic hair, you will probably find yourself either asking someone for a date or vice versa.

In this regard, you'll have two choices. One, you can date someone to whom you're not really attracted. This means you'll spend the evening with someone you don't really care about and your first date won't be much different from the rest of your life. Or two, you can elect to go on your first date with someone who makes your loins ache, palms sweat and mouth dry. This means your life will become an instant, living hell, because the odds are good that anyone who makes your loins ache, palms sweat and mouth dry will probably also make your bowels hot and runny. In public, this can be a problem.

Sooner or later, however, you will probably ask someone out on a date, and he or she will agree to go. This means you can start worrying about a whole lot of other stuff, such as a) how to comb your hair so that it hides the pimples on your forehead, b) how to suck in your stomach and still breath, and c) how much deodorant is enough. This biggest problem you face on a first date, however, is none of the above. It's what to talk about with your date. To prepare yourself for the expected awkwardness of your first private conversations, you may well spend days and weeks rehearsing chit chat, preparing soliloquies and practicing bits of clever dialogue in front of

26

your bedroom mirror. Despite these minutely preplanned conversations, however, once out for the evening, you and your date will probably discover that you have absolutely nothing to say to each other. Words will desert you. They will, in fact, seem to be foreign things, like stones or objects from another planet that drop from your mouth without order or meaning. In their arrant stupidity, they will make your lengthy silences all the more embarrassing. Before your date is over, you may well be astonished by the fact that two members of the same species from the same country on the same planet could share a common language and still have so little to discuss. Come to think of it, maybe this is why adolescents are confused. Maybe it's not breasts and pubic hair after all.

FIRST KISS (FEMALE)

You will go to a movie and spend the entire evening trying to keep your date's hands off any part of your body that's not identifiably your shoulder. Afterwards, your date will take you home. As you say "good night," your date will stammer briefly, then lunge at you, unaccountably, with eyes closed and tongue extended. If you're quick, alert and lucky, you will end up with little more than a damp spot on your dress. If you're not, this will be your first kiss. In either event, your date will later inform friends that he got to "third base."

FIRST KISS (MALE)

You will spend hours in a movie theater slipping your arm around the back of your date's seat with the ultimate goal of touching some part of her body which cannot be positively identified as her shoulder. Sometime during this effort, your arm will fall asleep and lose all feeling. Consequently, even if you do manage to touch something that cannot be positively identified as your date's shoulder, you will have no idea what it is. Afterwards you will take your date home, say "good night," maunder briefly on a subject of no importance and, moved by a passion beyond your accounting, lunge towards your date with eyes closed and tongue extended. If you're quick, this will be your first kiss. If not, you will end up licking the back of your date's dress. In either event, you will inform friends that you got to "third base."

FIRST SEXUAL EXPERIENCE

Everybody has a story to tell about his or her first sexual experience. Truthfully told, these stories are usually funny. In retrospect, at least. At the time, however, most first sexual experiences are like Hobbes' description of the life of the average seventeenth-century peasant as "nasty, short and brutish." Usually, the first sexual experience involves about equal amounts of physical pain and emotional discomfort. At any rate, it's nothing a normal person would call fun.

Given that fact, the most important thing you should do is pick a place that is, at least, comfortable. Traditional favorite trysting spots such as the back seat of the car, under the high school bleachers and far-flung corners of a corn field are clearly out of the question. These types of places are typically employed in ruttish desperation and usually chosen only because they're the only places you can be pretty sure your parents won't show up. Ideally, you should choose a place that is clean, dry and has a roof overhead. A seedy motel, for instance. While the experience itself will be no less miserable, at least you won't have stones in your back, bugs crawling up your nose and friends peeking in the car windows to watch. At any rate, let's be frank, just about any place beats a corn field.

THE PROM

The prom is the culmination of all the wonderful experiences you'll have in school. The fun begins months in advance when you start getting night sweats wondering whether anyone will go with you. In fact, someone probably will. It's not as if they really want to, of course, but remember, everyone else needs a date, too. Thus, by a process of elimination, you will eventually end up with a date of some kind. You see, it's virtually a law of nature that there are only ten to twelve people in any high school that everybody else wants to date. Invariably these people already have dates and wouldn't normally want to be seen with you unless you were actually in a position to save their lives, so don't even think about it. The rest of us have to settle for the leftovers—each other. What this means is that you will probably end up going to the prom with someone you're mildly embarrassed to be seen with, but hey, at least you'll be going.

At this point, you can start to worry about other things. Girls will worry about how they look. Boys will worry about how they can get into their date's pants. Thus, girls will spend a lot of money buying a dress. Boys will spend a lot of money on corsages and cheap liquor.

Finally, the big night will come! Within half an hour of arrival, girls will have danced until they have sweat rings under their arms and ruined their dresses. Boys will have drunk cheap liquor until they have thrown up on their tuxedoes and been threatened with suspension from school. On the way home from the prom you will either drive to a seedy motel and lose your virginity or drive into a concrete bridge abutment and lose your life. But hey, at least you went.

DRUGS

Despite adjurations to "just say 'no,'" everybody this side of the church social committee knows that sooner or later nine out of ten American adolescents say, "Well, maybe just once." However, the problem with most drugs is that they are, like most other reputed forms of fun, just about as enjoyable as sniffing old socks. Except, of course, that sniffing old socks is hardly ever addictive. Contrary to popular myth, you will not see God or anyone like Him. You will, however, frequently find yourself in a squalid part of town talking to some of the world's least interesting conversationalists: people who are, believe it or not, even more mind-numbing than most drugs. Anyway, here's the kind of fun you can expect to have.

POT

It'll make you cough. It'll make your eyes red. It'll make you paranoid. Your mother will want to know if you've been crying. OH NO! WHERE'D YOU LEAVE YOUR ROLLING PAPERS! IN THE KITCHEN?! It'll make you feel stupid and listen to Led Zepplin records. You'll be in a room with a "black light" that will make your zits glow in the dark. YIKES! WHAT ARE THEY!? I'VE GOT PURPLE THINGS ON MY FACE! Every time you pass a joint around, you'll get other people's lip boogies in your mouth. Yuck! Did you ever think about where those people's mouths have been? UGH! WHAT IF MOM FINDS YOUR ROLLING PAPERS?! YOU'LL BE GROUNDED FOREVER! BUMMER!

MIND-ALTERING CHEMICALS

You'll imagine you're omnipotent! You'll think you're God! You'll walk in front of a car to prove it. Then, all of a sudden: splat, oops, trip's over. And that's a good trip. On a bad one, you'll imagine stuff like your skin is turning into goat cheese, black blood is squirting out of your eyes and the police are holding your brain in a mayonnaise jar. The only way to stop it is to jump out the window. Whoooaaaa! Splat! Oops! Trip's over.

30

CRACK

You can ruin your mind a lot more cheaply by sniffing glue, so why go to the expense? Plus if you're anywhere near Washington D.C., you're likely to wind up in a room talking to Marion Barry. Why risk ruining your mind like that?

COCAINE

You can get about the same buzz by drinking three cups of strong coffee at about one-one thousandth of the cost. Worst of all, if you ever get addicted, there's a fifty-fifty chance you'll wind up whining about it in front of millions of people on "Oprah," "Geraldo," "The Donahue Show" or in a jail cell with Manuel Noreiga. Is this what you want out of life?

SPEED

Really, isn't life fast enough?

COLLEGE LIFE

College is a time eagerly anticipated by most people. This is because it's the time we can finally get away from our parents. Why parents consider paying $25,000 a year for this is an enigma. Maybe they want us out of the house as much as we want to go. At any rate, once in college, we are free to use our minds and explore our intellectual interests for, perhaps, the first time. Most of us opt not to do this since we are also free to use our bodies for, perhaps, the first time.

In short, rather than pursuing our studies, we pursue each other. In libraries, when we should be reading, we spend our time playing footsie. In lectures, when we should be listening, we spend our time winking. In laboratories, when we should be combining chemicals, we spend our time trying to determine if the chemistry is right with potential paramours. We take courses only because we know a certain special someone will be taking them, too. As a result, we study Art History instead of becoming lawyers as our parents had hoped. Later, to relax after the strain of our studies, we drink, dance and carouse. We submit papers late and $100,000 later, we receive diplomas. Years later, we wonder why the Japanese have taken over.

DORM LIFE

Some of our most ambitious students are driven to attend college in an effort to escape life in a slum. Then, they go live in a dorm and find themselves unable to tell the difference. People deal drugs in the hallways and urinate in the bushes. There are cockroaches in the bathrooms, the smell of greasy food is in the air and the incessant thump of loud music is everywhere. All this for just $25,000 a year. It makes you wonder what you'd get for $50,000.

ROOMMATES

On your first day at college, you'll be introduced to someone you'll dislike intensely. This will be your roommate. This person will be a somewhat fabled creature, your exact and total opposite. If you like to sleep late, he'll rise early. If you like to keep the room neat, she'll leave underwear hanging on the lamps. This may well be the only person in the universe with whom you'll have less in common than your parents. Funny, huh? Don't worry though, as a sophomore, you'll be allowed to choose your own roommate. Incidentally, this will be a person you'll like in September and loathe by June.

MIXERS

This is a queer name for an event you probably knew in high school as a dance. While the nomenclature is different, the procedure is pretty much the same: boys line up on one side, girls on the other. Each side points out the homelier members on the other and makes snide comments. Finally, someone you've been snickering about will cross the room and ask you to dance. Later, you may spend the evening together or perhaps, the night. Marriage is not out of the question.

FRAT PARTIES

Fraternity parties so often give the impression of being on a peculiar cul-de-sac of Hell, it's surprising to learn that Dante didn't reserve a special ring of the inferno for them. If you're a woman, frat parties are particularly galling, and there are a few things that you must keep in mind. One thing to remember is that frat parties are planned and attended by males who, until recently, have had their behavior closely monitored by their mothers. Second, remember that most frat men have only recently been permitted to drink alcoholic beverages in public and have only the vaguest idea of when to stop. Also keep in mind that they're all after just one thing. Sadly, this is not an education.

Consequently, at some point during any frat party, you should expect to be thrown on a couch while a frat member tries to thrust his tongue down your throat. Remember, this is his idea of foreplay and a mere prelude to assiduous efforts to get the one thing he's after. Also remember that a frat rat's concept of a dance consists largely of squirming on the floor in a large puddle of beer. And in general, keep in mind what people do to become members of these organizations. They tie each other up in unheated rooms, run through strange neighborhoods in rubber underwear and subject themselves to assorted weird rituals involving blindfolds, buckets of brine and bananas. Remember, too, that with few exceptions, the most extraordinary acts of idiocy ever conceived—from goldfish swallowing to telephone booth stuffing—were first envisioned by fraternity men. In short, this is their idea of fun. Are you sure you want to join them?

DRINKING GAMES

Parents send us off to college with the hope that we will spend most of our time struggling to fill our brains with knowledge. We, however, set off with the certain knowledge that we will spend most of our time casually filling our circulatory systems with alcohol and slaughtering our brain cells by the billions.

As you might expect of a nation weaned on video games and theme parks, college students are no longer simply content to sit across a table from one another and try to drink each other under it: they now have what are quaintly called drinking games. Those who lose these games will probably blow lunch. Those who win may well lapse into a coma. Fun, huh?

ATHLETIC EVENTS

At college athletic events, you will scream and cheer for semi-professional athletes under the pretense that they are your classmates. Of course, if they were really your classmates, you would occasionally expect to see one of them in one of your classes, wouldn't you? As far as you can tell, this has never happened. Incidentally, these athletes are the same kids who used to steal your lunch money during recess and beat you up on the way home from school. Why are you cheering?

STUDENT CLUBS

All through high school, kids get involved in clubs and organizations they wouldn't otherwise touch with a ten-foot pole because they think it will help them get into a good college. Hence, in high school, at least, belonging to an extracurricular organization is in some way understandable. Once in college, however, the impulse is harder to fathom. Why would anyone join an organization she didn't have to? Why would anyone congregate, on a regular basis, with people who weren't feeding her, clothing her or giving her money? In short, why would anyone choose to get involved in an extracurricular activity?

Some people, of course, have the same motivation they had in high school: they think it will look good on their resumes and help them land good jobs. After graduation, these people usually become politicians, insurance salesmen or someone else you'll want to keep out of your life. Other people who join collegiate clubs seem to be involved in a mysterious sort of typecasting. You see, invariably, anyone who willingly participates in an extracurricular activity is declaring herself in one way or another.

More than Rorschach tests or personality profiles, the extracurricular activities that college students join provide us with a deep insight into their personalities, their needs, desires and weaknesses. Not infrequently, joining one of these groups is a masked cry for help. In short, people who join college clubs under the guise that they're doing it for "fun" are really trying to tell you something. Consider the following messages that people in these clubs are sending you.

MARCHING BAND—No one's ever liked me. You don't have to listen, just don't boo.

DRAMA—I am deeply in love with myself, but I'm really not sure if I want to be a boy or a girl. Would you like to watch while I figure this out?

LEFT-WING POLITICAL ORGANIZATION—I have no idea what I'm going to do for a living. My parents went to Woodstock.

RIGHT-WING POLITICAL ORGANIZATION—My dad's a jerk. So am I.

MOVIE CLUB—My father donated the money for the new gym. No matter how long it takes me to graduate, I still don't intend to do anything while I'm here.

FOREIGN LANGUAGE SOCIETY—I like to talk a lot, but I'm not sure people like to listen. Maybe if I try a different language....?

This Is God's Image?
Pleasures of the Flesh

SEX

Formerly, sex was something to feel guilty about, which made it meaningful, satisfying and enjoyable. Then came the sexual revolution which told us that sex was fun and instantly transformed it from an unspeakable sin into unremitting drudgery. Soon it became requisite to try positions which could only benefit chiropodists. After awhile, normal housewives had mirrors installed on their bedroom ceilings and discovered the only difference it made was that they could now count the zits on their husbands' backs during intercourse. Now, half the population is afraid of AIDS, while the other half lives in fear of genital warts. In short, the natural order has been ruined and things are a mess; all because of our misbegotten pursuit of fun.

Come on now, folks, if God had really wanted sex to be fun, why are human bodies engineered so that the male is a bubbling broth of hormones at exactly the same age that the female is erotically aroused as easily as a beach blanket? The inescapable conclusion is that sex is something you'll enjoy much more if you just do it by yourself. Consider the following:

- If you do it in the morning, the kids will come in and ask what's for breakfast.

- If you do it at night, you'll miss the best TV shows.

- If you do it with a new sexual partner, you'll find yourself thinking about (a) herpes (b) syphilis or (c) AIDS.

- If you do it with your usual sexual partner you'll find yourself thinking about (a) stocks and bonds (b) the laundry or (c) someone else.

- If you're trying to conceive a child, having sex will be about as much fun as taking out the garbage.

- If you're not trying to conceive a child, you may well be committing a sin.

- Sooner or later you may experience a great deal of anxiety about your ability to perform. The more you think about it, the worse it will get. The worse it gets, the more you will think about it. Before it's all over, you could write a book like Phillip Roth.

- Sooner or later you may experience a great deal of anxiety about your partner's ability to perform. The more you think about it, the worse it will get. The worst it gets, the more you will think about it. Before it's all over, you could write a book like Dr. Joyce Brothers.

- Your partner will be someone who doesn't know the first thing about sex. Sex will be cold, mechanical and ruin your life.

- Your partner will be an insatiable maniac who will buy a sex manual and want to perform every act, page by page, every time you get in bed. Sex will be hot, sweaty and ruin your sheets.

Besides, God is watching.

NUDE BEACH

As you walk away from a nude beach, you will realize the only good thing about it is that you don't have sand in your bathing suit. See, while most people are lured to nude beaches by the prospect of seeing nude men and women who look like Daryl Hannah and Mel Gibson, what they typically see are nude men and women who look like Roseanne Barr and John Goodman; in other words, people with revolting tufts of hair on their shoulder blades, who long ago abandoned the notion that holding in their stomachs was of the slightest consequence. You see, the veils of illusion regarding the unclothed human form are quickly stripped away along with our vestments. What we are actually exposed to on a nude beach is the most basic, grim stark naked truth about humanity: without clothes on, we all look like plucked chickens and should seriously consider setting aside a day just to celebrate the invention of slacks.

At a nude beach, males, in particular, face some rather thorny problems. One is that small eels are what large fish eat. So if you go in the water, be careful. As a male, you also face the serious question of whether to carry a paperback book in front of your unmentionables. If you do, of course, other people on the beach will assume you're either (a) a voyeur or (b) hung like a hamster. If you don't, you face the painful prospect of getting the most agonizing sunburn of your life. Finally, let's remember that this kind of behavior is precisely why Adam and Eve were expelled from the Garden. Why tempt fate?

HEALTH CLUBS

Not since the Spanish Inquisition has there been such a flourishing of equipment devoted to inflicting human pain as we now find in health clubs; even the grunts, groans and moans recall those ancient chambers of pain. The difference is that nowadays we willingly strap ourselves into these bizarre machines instead of being forced into them under duress.

I ask you, how did this happen? How is it possible that a thinking public could ever be persuaded to believe that anything as elementally disagreeable as exercise could be considered, in any way, enjoyable? The only conceivable answers are that (a) a thinking public does not exist or (b) we've all succumbed to an exotic brainwashing technique Jane Fonda acquired in North Vietnam. Subsequently, in imitation of rodents on treadmills, we now walk mile after perspiring mile without going anywhere. We squeeze our buttocks in response to the irksome exhortations of bumptious, bouncing, brainless beach bunnies. We assume positions reminiscent of extreme sexual compromise while bound with leather straps in chromium machines. We develop shin splints, stress fractures and fallen arches. We induce water on the knee and severe coronary events; all this in an arena redolent of old gym socks.

Some of us even become body builders. First, please let us remember that lifting heavy objects is not why man was created; lifting heavy objects is why the steam engine was created. Putatively, body builders are making themselves look more attractive to the opposite sex. In actuality, however, they are making themselves look more like the opposite sex. Male body builders develop large pectoral lumps on their chests while steroids shrink their testicles to the size of black-eyed peas. Female body builders develop large muscle masses and grotesque, bulging veins. Ultimately they look more like men than most males. And they wonder why it's hard to get a date?

Of course, exercise can give you a temporarily better-looking body and help you feel marginally better as you get older. Recent medical research, however, proves that exercise won't help you live longer. But who'd want to live longer, anyway? It would only mean you'd have to exercise more.

SINGLES BARS

If you ever see someone having a good time at a singles bar, you may feel confident that person is either (a) the owner or (b) married. For single men and women, singles bars offer only two disappointing prospects: (1) spending the night with someone who would disgust you if you were sober, and (2) utter, crushing, never-to-be forgotten rejection. If you're a male, you will be treated with contempt by women who, in the last five years, have not had a single thought that didn't directly concern styling gel. If you're a female, you will be appraised with disdain by men who are genetically incapable of buttoning their shirts all the way to the top.

Nonetheless, sooner or later, someone will try to cajole you into accompanying him to a singles bar. If you have the slightest suspicion that this person may be better looking than yourself, do not go. The only reason this so-called friend invited you is to make him look better by comparison or to drive him home if he gets drunk.

If, through boredom or weakness, however, you allow yourself to be coerced into going to a singles bar, here's what will happen:

- No one will talk to you.

- No one will dance with you.

- During the first half hour, you will eat enough free pretzels to get sodium poisoning.

- You will start drinking to "get loose." Before the evening's over, you will be so "loose" you will have lost your car keys and forgotten where you live.

Other than that, just remember that conversation in a singles bar is a nervous reaction much like a knee twitch and has nothing at all to do with the exchange of ideas. In fact, the main function of talking in a singles bar is just so people can check out each other's breath. So don't worry much about what you're saying, just make sure to use mouthwash before you go. Besides, most of the people you'll run into never did their own homework once in their entire lives, so exactly what do you expect to talk to them about anyway? Nuclear physics?

DANCING

When it comes to dancing, the ranks of humanity are divided along strictly sexual lines: women love to dance while men hate it. Men hate it because they feel it's a silly, pointless activity which, if done well, will expose them to charges of effeminacy. (Women, of course, don't have to be afraid of charges of effeminacy. After all, what would be the point?) At any rate, men frequently find themselves induced to dance by women who, by the age of fourteen, have gotten sick and tired of dancing with each other.

Typically, women get men out on the dance floor by promising them it will be fun. Where women get this idea, no one is quite sure. Clearly, they don't get it from watching men dance. The most plausible theory is that women get this idea from watching movies of Fred Astaire. Unfortunately, what women tend to forget is that most men don't dance like Fred Astaire. What most men dance like are blindfolded bears in leg irons.

Nonetheless, as women step out onto the dance floor, they are often smiling. This is because they harbor fond, romantic notions of whisking about the floor as lightly as feathers wafted about in a breeze. On the other hand, as men step onto the dance floor, they are almost uniformly grim and disagreeable. This is largely because the thought of doing anything a woman wants them to do makes them that way.

Soon after a dance starts, however, the female dance partner is usually about as miserable as the male. This is because her fond, romantic notion, has been shattered by a brutal reality. Instead of being wafted about like a feather in a zephyr, she has, almost invariably, found herself kicked, clomped and thrown about in a random fashion with little regard for bumps, bruises, broken bones or her personal safety. Thus, typically, a dance ends not when a song is over, but when the partners begin arguing about who's not leading and both will stomp angrily off the dance floor in opposite directions. You see, while dancing is thought by many to be a leisure-time activity and a mild form of exercise, it's actually just one more example of the virtually unbreachable gulf between what men and women find enjoyable.

The Outdoors:
What's So Great About It?

CAMPING

When we think of camping, we typically think of things like making friends with the Indians, using the sun to guide us through the forests and wrasslin' bears with our bare hands. In short, camping is one of the great romantic delusions of our lives. Please let us recall that *The Boy Scout Manual* is filled with chapters explaining tourniquets, splints, amputation, artificial respiration, gangrene and why you're dumb if you don't carry a snakebite kit. Now let me ask you, you don't think they put this stuff in there as some curious form of amusement, do you? No. Sadly, this is what you can expect if you go camping. In return for surviving this sort of suffering, we are promised that we will discover the beauty of nature as well as unknown inner resources. What we typically discover on a camping trip, however, is why man invented motels, electric blankets and hide away beds in the first place. What's more, just as there are immutable laws of nature, there are also unchanging canons of camping. The first of these is that you will forget to bring something critical to your comfort or crucial to your survival: a canteen, a compass or clean socks.

The second canon states that any equipment you bring is likely to fail at the worst possible time. In the middle of a rain storm, for instance, the tent will collapse; in the middle of the night the air mattress will deflate; and in the middle of a blizzard, your matches will be damp and useless. Furthermore, if a piece of equipment doesn't fail you, it will probably injure you. A gas stove, for instance, will explode, a kerosene lantern will ignite, and due to the astonishing multiplicity of possibilities, the single attempt to use a Swiss Army knife can leave you not only sliced, but also snipped, gouged, notched, sawn, perforated, punched, awl-holed and corkscrewed.

Third, you will find that a campfire, even if you can manage to get one started, is completely useless. Employ one to dry your expensive, new boots, and they will end up looking like large, leather potato chips. Try to cook on one, and everything will be burnt on the outside, while remaining virtually frozen on the inside. Attempt to warm yourself by a campfire in the winter, and you will find that only those parts of your body which are not actually ablaze will feel anything other than frozen.

Finally, that fourth canon simply states that if you go camping with others, you will come to despise them. If you go camping by yourself, you will break your leg in a fall and die waiting for help. Now there's something the Boy Scouts didn't tell you about.

HUNTING

"The unspeakable in pursuit of the uneatable."

Oscar Wilde on fox hunting

Hunters are people who will expound on the beauty of animals, line their dens with decoys, etchings and paintings of the creatures, and then go out and blow them apart with no apparent compunction. So what can we expect from them? Certainly not rational thought, which is undoubtedly why some of them consider hunting an enjoyable pastime. If you ever go hunting, here's what you can expect in the way of enjoyment.

For starters, you will sit in the woods on a miserable day. If an animal wanders by, you will raise your gun and shoot at it. If you miss, the animal may charge and maul you. It's not mere speculation to suppose that the reason they call certain bears "grizzlies" is because of the kind of murders they commit. On the other hand, if you don't miss, you will have to take the animal home and eat it. Often it's hard to determine which eventuality is less desirable.

Typically, wild game tastes like something you've already eaten. I don't mean like chicken, either. I mean like something you've swallowed and thrown up. Take, for instance, wild duck. Despite the fact that after you've dressed and cooked it, a wild duck is hardly larger than a welterweight moth, you'll find most people will have trouble eating the whole thing. Usually after a dinner of wild duck, you will discover most guests have furtively fed it to the dog or stealthily spat every bite into a napkin. In any event, your dog is probably the only one who will actually enjoy eating a wild duck. But remember, that's something he's been bred for over the course of hundreds of years.

Your guests' disgust, however, is not entirely due to the foul taste of wild meat. To a large extent, it's because of the inevitable association people will make between the greasy carcass you've laid before them and certain, precious memories of youth. Need I mention Donald, Daisy and Daffy or Huey, Dewey and Louie? Who could enjoy gnawing on the butchered remains of these beloved cartoon characters? And dare I mention Bambi? The mere sight of venison is frequently enough to evoke memories of one's first, tragic tears. And if sensitive diners don't weep, they well may laugh. Who could put moose on the table without anticipating the inevitable mention of Bullwinkle and the attendant impressions that are sure to last throughout the meal? How could you ask people to eat beaver without expecting to become a laughingstock yourself? In short, when you serve wild meat, you can expect to become a target yourself—of outrage, derision and contempt. This is fun?

FISHING

Hemingway once said the only thing he really liked about fishing was that it provided an excuse to drink before breakfast. The truth is that most of the time fishing is a lot like sitting around the house, except you happen to be doing it near water with a pole in your hand. Typically, of course, you won't catch anything or even get a nibble, which is fine, because it's a great chance to enjoy a nice day without having anybody wonder why you're not doing something socially significant.

The fact of the matter is that, these days, there just aren't that many fish out there. In truth, you're much more likely to see medical waste and discarded syringes floating around in the water than a fish; and the only time you can reasonably expect to have something alive on the end of your line is when you use live bait. Using live bait, however, will require you to dig up grubs, handle slugs and fondle night crawlers. It also means you'll have to pull sharpened barbs through the lips of innocent minnows and impale the wriggling, writhing bodies of worms on hooks while watching their gooey guts ooze forth from their punctured forms. Who could enjoy this? Presumably only those who, as children, took exceptional delight in tormenting cats and pulling the wings from captured insects.

The other basic method of not catching fish, of course, is with artificial lures such as plugs, dry flies, spinners, spoons and so forth. In general, an artificial lure may be defined as something that will remind a fish of nothing he's ever seen before. In fact, it seems to me that the number of fish actually caught with lures is roughly equal to the number of fish which could be expected to commit suicide. In other words, you're not really deceiving a fish with a lure, you're merely providing it with a convenient way of ending a damp and miserable life. All in all, fishing with lures is pretty much a confessed waste of time. There are, however, some fisherman who claim that what they really enjoy about fishing is the art of tying dry flies. Basically, this means they're willing to devote a lot of time and effort to making something that may give a fish the impression it's looking at a mosquito. Is this really a good use of a limited life span?

While all these methods of angling are about as equally unproductive, there may, nonethess, come a time when you actually catch a fish. In this rare event, you face the gruesome prospect of cleaning it. This means you will have to scrape off the fish's scales, slice open its stomach, pull out its guts and chop off its head. By the time you're finished, you will smell a lot like the fish itself, with piquant undertones of the bait you used and subtle overtones of a dock. Consequently, when you go home, don't be surprised if your family greets you, not with open arms and shouts of joyous admiration but rather with pinched nostrils and gagging exhortations to use the shower. As for the fish, no one will want to eat it; not your family, neighbors, relatives or cat. Congratulations.

HIKING

What is the most annoying part of hiking? Is it the horrid thought you will tramp up and down until your feet bleed, your legs cramp and back aches? Is it the knowledge you will be surrounded by gnats, assaulted by biting flies and will reach your destination too exhausted to enjoy the much vaunted view? Or is it the hideous likelihood that you may have to listen to one of your cohorts sing several hundred verses of "The Bear Went Over the Mountain"? At any rate, it's hard to imagine what the real pleasure of hiking is. You will merely walk through mud and over rough terrain, tripping on roots and rocks, exposing yourself to ticks and, ultimately, the agonies of Rocky Mountain spotted fever and Lyme Tick disease. You will return from a hike with tootsies that have been rubbed red and raw and that are in rather immediate need of podiatric attention. In short, despite the promises of naturalists, you will not experience bliss while hiking. Merely blisters.

SPELUNKING

First of all, let's remember that caves are where bats live. Why would anyone in his right mind visit a bat at home? Besides, what comes closer to illustrating Freud's hypothesis regarding the death wish than crawling around in a cave? Just think: there you are beneath the ground, entombed in darkness, surrounded by dirt and, typically, confined to a space not much larger than an actual crypt. And why? To look at dirt and mud with a flashlight? To wriggle on one's belly over bat guano? To find a few rocks that could easily be purchased at a nearby souvenir stand? To become friends with salamanders and spiders? Or is it merely to feel the questionable thrill of claustrophobia and imminent suffocation?

CANOEING

Paddling a canoe is probably the closest you can come to enjoying water without actually mixing scotch in it, but there are still drawbacks. One is called portaging. This is a euphemism and like all euphemisms, it's an attempt to mask a lot of misery with a misleading word. You see, "portaging" simply means "carrying" and what you're carrying is the canoe. What's worse is that in most places where you have to carry the canoe, it's hard enough just to walk. Usually, for instance, you have to portage your canoe around a rapid which means you'll have to walk up a steep bank, through a dense forest, over a lot of sharp rocks and side by side with about half the world's mosquito population to get where you're going. Clearly, no fun.

Another thing that's clearly no fun is canoeing into the wind, which, when you think about it, you'll probably have to do about half the time. This is when you'll discover just how similar a canoe is to a sailboat without a sail. The wind will simply push you and your canoe wherever it wants to, despite the fact that you will paddle until you get blisters. Speaking of blisters, it's generally the chump in the front of a canoe who gets all of them while the guy in the back loafs along pretending to steer. At any rate, when you get into a canoe, make sure you get in back. If you go over a waterfall, at least you won't go first.

GARDENING

Typically, gardening is about as enjoyable as cleaning an old stove, while conferring upon its practitioners a few of that activity's immediately gratifying and tangible results. For some inscrutable reason, however, gardening is becoming more and more popular, chic and trendy. Believe me, I can smell it in the air, not to mention in the piles of rotted manure that my neighbors are having dumped on their lawns, with a frequency that's alarming to everyone but the owners of nearby nurseries.

But before you start saving eggshells and coffee grounds for the compost heap and debating the merits of 0-10-10 fertilizer versus 5-10-5 fertilizer, there are a few things to consider. First, almost every revolution in the history of man has been waged by people who were fed up with just the sort of labor we now quaintly call "puttering around the garden." How it's possible to feel the least bit chic when you're grubbing around in the dirt, spreading animal feces with your hands and generally performing the same sort of dreary toil that's traditionally been pawned off on slaves, serfs and other unfortunate bumpkins is beyond me. Apparently, however, that's just what's happening to a lot of young, suburban types who are now rooting through the soil in their backyards like trained pigs hot on the trail of a truffle instead of staying inside, where they belong, digging for truffles in their pâté. Besides which, what do these gardeners usually grow, anyway? Despite assiduous efforts to make bulbs sprout, shrubs thrive and lawns flourish, the only thing most people succeed in raising is weeds. Clearly, weeds were meant to sprout, thrive and flourish on this gnarled, little planet. Nothing else was. So why fight the trend?

There are, of course, a few exceptions, things any gardener can grow easily and in abundance. Mostly cucumbers, squash and zucchini. These grow in such extraordinary profusion, in fact, it's hard to even get rid of them. During the zucchini harvesting season, for instance, anyone growing these vegetative tumors will inevitably show up at your doorstep with a bag full. "Take some zucchini," he will beg. "No thanks, I just got a half ton from someone else," you will probably answer. He will then resort to making zucchini bread, zucchini loaf and zucchini salad. For all you know, he'll even make hats and loafers out of the stuff. You see, the simple truth is that when vegetables like zucchini, squash, cucumbers, even corn and tomatoes, are in season, you can get all you want for free from the dimwits who've bothered to plant them. At the most, they'll cost twenty cents a pound at the store, which is approximately two dollars per pound less than they cost to grow.

Last, I think we should all remember that one of God's initial acts, after the creation of man, was to express His contempt for gardening and His disgust with garden products. I mean, if God doesn't care about gardening, why should you?

PICNICS

A picnic is rarely a picnic. Even in its most perfect imaginable form—the sort of idyllic scene Watteau might have imagined—it's still a classic example of the inevitable clash between human beings and the rest of the planet. I'm not referring to the prosaic occurrences such as an attack by ants to see who will get to your potato salad first or an assault by mosquitoes to see who will go home with the greater portion of your blood.

I'm speaking of the absolute inevitability of the fact that, whenever you sit on the ground, whether you spread a picnic blanket or not, sooner or later, nature's most mysterious form of moisture will rise from the earth, penetrate the blanket, permeate your pants and uncomfortably dampen your underwear. Where does this moisture come from? Look at the ground and you can't see it. Put your hand to the earth and you can't feel it. But sit down and suddenly, as if from nowhere, it will be there (perhaps for the first time since you wore diapers), making you wriggle, writhe, squirm and itch; forcing you to stealthily, but constantly, readjust your undergarments when you think nobody's looking.

But, of course, this is not the only insidious attack that nature launches. Even on a perfectly clear day, with no wind and not a bird or tree in sight, you go on a picnic with the certain knowledge that inexplicable chunks of unidentifiable crud will wind up floating in your cup of lemonade. What are these chunks? Bellybutton lint from a passing bird? Tree bark? And where do they come from? Miniature asteroids? Perhaps, but who knows? It's all just part of the implacable battle waged since time immemorial between man and nature, and on a picnic nature clearly has the upper hand.

That is not to say that all the disasters on a picnic will be due to natural causes. On any picnic, a minimum of one gamboling child will cut his foot on a rusted can, requiring stitches and a tetanus booster shot. On any picnic, a minimum of one food item, commonly made with mayonnaise, will give a minimum of two picnickers food poisoning. On a picnic, even the way you eat is a problem. For instance, do you really think that at some point during the meal a paper plate isn't going to disintegrate in your hands and dump beans all over your loafers? Do you really think that at some time a hamburger is not going to squeeze out of its bun and wind up on the ground? Do you really think you're going to squeeze a ketchup bottle and not have it wind up with a gory-looking splotch on your pants? Come on, get serious. Even under the best of circumstances, a picnic is just more proof of why man first conceived of the dining room.

Sports:
Blood, Sweat and Tears, but Mostly Sweat

BOWLING

Bowling is a lot like masturbation. It's a lot of fun, but not necessarily something you want to admit to in public. Bowling, unfortunately, suffers from a social stigma which is almost indefinable, yet unshakeable and probably dates back to the days when it was called kegling and indulged in, almost exclusively, by guys whose breath smelled like bratwurst and cigars even right after they'd brushed their teeth. Even its detractors, however, must admit that there are two great things about bowling: (1) you can get as drunk as you want and still do just about as well as you would if you were sober, and (2) you don't have to chase your own balls.

While bowling is a relatively benign pastime which keeps a lot of borderline sociopaths involved in something constructive on nights they might otherwise be breaking into your house, it's not without hazard. The main hazard in bowling, of course, is dropping the ball on your foot. I have an aunt who does this about once a year; it never gets any easier for her to explain that she's wearing a cast because she was lining up a turkey split and just happened to let a twelve-pound piece of Bakelite plummet onto her toes. Worse yet, with a bowling injury, you don't even have the solace you have in skiing, of being able to concoct some fallacious tale of bravado and derring-do, which will impress others and assuage the pain. When you hurt yourself bowling, people just laugh, and there's nothing you can do about it.

At any rate, if you want to bowl on a regular basis, you should probably buy your own equipment. After all, if you don't have your own shoes and ball, you'll just have to use what they've got in the alley. This means you'll have to stick your fingers in the holes of a ball that's recently been used by someone who unquestionably picks his nose; and you'll have to wear shoes that have just been on someone else's feet. Come to think of it, no wonder this sport has a social stigma.

GOLF

"Golf is a good walk, ruined."

Mark Twain

The only time you'll see a golfer smile is shortly before he takes his first shot or shortly after he's watched someone else hit into a sand trap. The rest of the time he will look like he's trying to pass a particularly agonizing kidney stone, which should give you some clue as to how much fun golf is. I mean, face it duffers, would you really spend the day muttering foul, filthy curses and calling yourself a "worthless son of a bitch" if you were enjoying yourself? Just think, if Scotland had had nice beaches, golf might never have been invented. Besides, Ike Eisenhower, the Commander-in-Chief of the Allied armies during World War II and President of the most powerful nation on earth, flailed at a golf ball every opportunity he had, never coming close to par. So what chance do you think you have? At any rate, by the time a round of golf is over, your feet will hurt and you will have undergone a predictable and well-documented series of miseries. At least once a round, for instance, you can expect to hit a putt that will go as far as your best drive; and, at least once a round, you can expect to hit a drive that will go no further than your worst putt. Furthermore, any time you try to impress someone who's watching, you will (a) slice the ball into the woods (b) hook the ball into a pond, or (c) miss the ball completely and dislocate something in your lumbar region.

As any triathlete will remind you, however, golf can hardly be considered a sport. After all, how can you really consider something that requires less physical conditioning than a board game, encourages its adherents to ride around in silly, little carts and is chiefly played by people who haven't been able to see or touch their toes in years a sport? (What would you call the fungal infection golfers get between their toes anyway? Non-athlete's foot?)

However, this does not mean you can't get hurt in golf. The main dangers are (a) getting hit by lightning from above (b) getting hit by a ball driven from behind, or (c) getting hit with the bar bill when you're done. In regard to "b," remember that if you ever do get hit by a golf ball, it's unquestionably a mistake. If a golfer had really been aiming at you, he would have missed.

TENNIS THE MENACE AND OTHER RACQUET SPORTS

It was while playing tennis that the seventeenth-century Italian painter Caravaggio killed someone. I forget whether it was his partner or an opponent, but in either case I'm sure he had good reason. Tennis is one of the most infuriating activities that can be undertaken by a human. For years, you will flail away at the ball and succeed only in hitting it into the net or over the fence into somebody's backyard. Finally, after about a decade of this humiliation, you will be good enough to hit it over the net without hitting it into somebody's backyard. At this point, you will have tennis elbow which can't be cured and isn't even covered by Blue Cross. You will also discover that, no matter how good you get, there are three immutable rules of tennis:

- **Any time you hit an overhead, it will go into the net.**

- **Any time you have an easy shot, you will hit it out.**

- **Any time someone is watching, you will miss the ball entirely.**

However, the real problem with tennis often has less to do with the difficulty of hitting the ball and more to do with the difficult people who play. Remember John McEnroe? Let's also remember that you'll normally have to rely on your opponent to honestly and accurately call shots "in" or "out." In a society rife with used car dealers and door-to-door encyclopedia sales people–a society which has furthermore twice elected Richard Nixon to our highest office–we all know what happens when we rely on anyone's honesty. Any time your opponent needs a point, he will simply lie. No wonder people throw racquets.

Remember also there are really only two places you can play tennis. One is at a public court. At public facilities, most players will spend more time hitting balls into your court than they will into their own. Furthermore, because public courts don't cost anything, they're usually crowded. Thus, if you want to play more than once every geologic period, you'll have to join a country club. In this case, there are two things to remember: 1) they probably won't let you in, and 2) if they do, you'll have to pay an enormous amount of money for the privilege of playing with people who will never tire of trying to prove that they're better than you both on the court and off. Dealing with social snubs and petty snobbery will, consequently, become as much a part of your life as jock itch and tennis toe. If you come from an ethnic background, your family will be scorned, your friends disparaged and your surname subjected to ridicule. Thus, even if you become a reasonably good tennis player, you'll still have to consider yourself a failure on some more irremediable level.

Finally remember that if you take up tennis, you're participating in one of the few sports other than figure skating in which people will assume you have a vague desire to defect to the opposite sex. If you're a male, people will figure your parents gave you a tennis racquet just to keep you from playing with dolls. If you're a female, they'll all be waiting for a moustache to sprout. As if, merely hitting the ball into the net nine times out of ten wasn't humiliation enough.

PING PONG

At the mere mention of ping pong, most people summon up a vision of paddles with the rubber padding half chewed off by an undisciplined dog, a mildewed basement and a ball that looks like a cuckoo's egg. Is this why this sport is so hard to take seriously? Or is it that the best practitioners are earnest nerds whacking a spherical egg off a piece of green plywood at an absurd distance from each other. The only good thing about it is that it's hard to imagine playing ping pong and getting injured. After all, what's going to happen to you even if you get hit by the ball? The yolk will fall out? Come on.

BADMINTON

While it may be hard to take ping pong seriously, it's almost impossible to keep a straight face when talking about a game played with something called a shuttlecock. One hesitates to mention the object of play in mixed company. Even if you can overcome this adolescent preoccupation, you must admit that this dainty, delicate object, looking like nothing more than the road-killed remains of an infant tern, does little to assert badminton's right to be called a sport.

SQUASH

Once again the nomenclature. Are you speaking of a sport or a vegetable? Unless circumstances make it clear, one never knows.

THE DISCONTENTS
OF OUR WINTER

In a desperate and rather pathetic attempt to relieve the bleakness and boredom of winter in the chillier parts of our planet, someone often suggests one of the following winter activities. While many of these pursuits sound good in the abstract, in reality they typically turn out to be some sort of gelid version of hell.

DOWNHILL SKIING

This is one of the most highly promoted and avidly pursued of all "fun" activities, which should give you a clue to the fact that it's just about as much fun as being buried alive. Of course, this is not entirely out of the question. Avalanches, remember?

Downhill skiing is also a sport in which the competition is intense, in this case, mainly to see (a) who can afford the most expensive outfits, and (b) who can get a parking space within a day's walk of the ski slope. Incidentally, no matter how sleek, chic and expensive your clothes are, if you ever take them off to use the bathroom in the lodge, you will find it impossible to get dressed again in a manner that will feel comfortable. Your underwear will pinch, bind and become twisted around your legs in a way that's oddly disconcerting and impossible to correct. Personally, I attribute many otherwise unaccountable skiing accidents to this common occurence.

Once you're out on the slopes, however, you will forget entirely about the hassle and expense of skiing. This is because you have much more immediate concerns involving self-preservation. For instance, every so often, you will find yourself approached by a pastel blur. This will be a seven-year-old child going approximately 100 MPH, who has no intention of stopping, even if you get in his way, and no means of stopping, if he had the intention. Due to his youth, he will probably survive any collision you two should have. Your chances aren't so good. Unfortunately, on ski slopes, these kids are all but inescapable nowadays.

On other occasions, you may find yourself being approached by something large and white. This is the aforementioned avalanche. On a ski slope, these never are escapable. Your chances of survival here are nil. Typcially, however, you will find yourself being approached by something tan, followed by something shrieking. This will be a member of the ski patrol hauling the mangled form of someone with a broken leg. Despite his obvious pain, you will consider this person lucky. This is because he already knows, more or less, what the extent of his injuries will be by the time he gets to the bottom of the mountain. You, on the other hand, still have no idea.

CROSS-COUNTRY SKIING

You'll discover it's very much like....no, no it's exactly like walking through the snow with Venetian blinds strapped to your feet. Even the negligible pleasures of downhill skiing don't pertain.

ICE SKATING PARTIES

These parties are opportunities for people to get together and complain about how cold it is. Without exception, ice skating parties are enjoyed most by those who fall through the ice and go home early.

SNOWMOBILING

Snowmobiling is perhaps the ultimate proof of man's uncontrollable passion for burning gasoline whenever and wherever he can. Now, we finally have the opportunity to imbue the tranquillity, serenity and solitude of a snowy forest with all the beauty, grandeur and majesty of a go-kart track. Great.

SLEDDING

This is perhaps the only method of locomotion ever devised without any means of directing the vehicle or controlling its speed. Considering that we encourage our children to go sledding down steep hills at speeds of up to 30 MPH–face down–with their teeth mere inches from hard-packed glare ice, does it really make sense to invest thousands of dollars in orthodontia?

ICE FISHING

Come on, cut it out, will you? Where exactly does one find pleasure in handling a wet, slimey, squirming creature when the weather is windy, cold and miserable. I don't even want to talk about it anymore.

SAILING:
OVER THE BORING MAIN

Clearly the people who enjoy sailboats most are those who leave them tied to the dock and use them as floating foundations on which to have parties, get drunk and watch sunsets. These people, however, are invariably sneered at by those who consider themselves members of the sailing fraternity. You see, much like buying the right suit, an expensive car or a house in a neighborhood you can't really afford, sailing is not so much an activity to be enjoyed, as an exercise in social one-upmanship. This fact may be deduced from the very language of the sport , which is one of the most patent attempts to linguistically separate oneself from the masses since the priests of Egypt pointedly refused to teach anyone else to read. The left, for instance, is not called "the left," it's called "the port"; furthermore, the right is called "the starboard", and never the twain shall meet, except once at the bow and again at the stern. What's more, there's also a leech, a luff, a halyard, a tack and a clew; not that anybody who's not a member of the sailing set will have a clue as to what any of these things are, which is really the whole point of this obscurantism. It allows anyone who sails to quickly and simply distinguish himself from anyone who doesn't and to start sneering at him without wasting any time.

The main thing to consider about sailboats is that they're so slow it's almost un-American. Furthermore after you sail out into the sunset, sooner or later you're going to have to turn around and come back; and you'll still be going just as slow. Let's keep in mind that sportswriters typically compare watching a twelve-meter yacht race to watching the grass grow, and twelve-meter boats are among the fastest sailboats in the world. In fact, if you could walk on water, there's a good chance you'd be going faster than most sailboats, and this may well explain why Jesus was never seen on a catamaran.

By the way, God forbid you should ever get involved in racing a sailboat. First of all, you'll find yourself being shrieked at by some suburban version of Captain Bligh with zinc oxide on his nose. Second, unlike other sports, a sailboat race isn't even over when it's over. As soon as it's over, there are invariably endless protests, challenges and general quibbling, until the entire event becomes little more than a wet, frothy version of small claims court. Ironically, people claim they enjoy sailboat racing, because it lets them get away from the arguments, tensions and petty pressures of the workaday world. Then, once on the water, they reproduce the arguments tensions and petty pressures of the workaday world in minute detail, except with wet feet. Go figure.

Finally, remember that no matter what anybody who sells you a sailboat says, you'll have to scrape it and paint it every year plus increase the amount you worry about hurricanes, typhoons and water spouts by an exponential factor. And all for what? So people you hardly know and relatives you'd rather not see can invite themselves out for a cruise every weekend? Hey, if you really want to see these people, you don't have to go to the expense of buying a sailboat. The promise of a free hamburger or wienie will usually do the trick, so why not just get yourself a hibachi?

WATER SKIING

In the seventeenth century, the Puritans devised a quaint New England custom called "dunking," in which a person was tied to a chair, plunged into water and held there until he finally said whatever our forefathers wanted to hear; which was, usually a confession that you were a witch or a close, personal friend of one. I mention this because it's not too different from what you will experience when you first learn to waterski.

While still safely on the boat, you will, of course, express natural reservations about (a) being run over by the boat and turned into chopped liver by the propellor, and (b) getting dragged by the towrope and receiving a high-speed, seventy-five gallon saltwater enema without the benefit of an attendant nurse. Your misgivings will be summarily dismissed, however, by people who don't seem to have given these matters much thought. "Those things never happen," they will say as they strap two large boards to your feet and push you overboard.

Once in the water, you will have cause to reflect on the fact that you now look very much like a large basking seal and that large basking seals are what sharks eat. In fact, it may well occur to you that there are lots of things swimming around out there that will remain unseen and unknown until they actually start to eat you, such as sea snakes, snapping turtles, moray eels and narwhales. Oddly enough, these creatures will not be your main concern. Your main concern will be breathing. You see, the first time you go waterskiing is one of those times in your life when you will have little control over your body or your destiny. You will simply bob about at the whim of the wind and tide–choking, coughing and sputtering–while your lungs and sinus passages fill with water. Nonetheless, you will finally drift into a position that will bear some resemblance to the one required to achieve a successful take-off. At this point, the people on the boat will ask a strictly rhetorical question: "Are you ready?" Remembering that "ready" is the word used shortly before "aim" and "fire" during executions, you will voice your objections. Despite these pleas, the person driving the boat will gun the engine and off you will go.

Under normal circumstances, of course, the towrope will be yanked from your grasp and, within nanoseconds, you will be back in the water–choking, coughing and sputtering. It may, in fact, be surmised that the nanosecond was first conceived as a means of measuring the length of time a human can actually waterski during a first attempt. At this point, your disgruntled acquaintances on board the boat will exhort you to "keep your knees together," "keep your tips up," "keep your arms bent" and generally offer all sorts of waterskiing advice and lore that's utterly useless to anyone, such as yourself, who's busy drowning.

In rare instances, of course, you may actually pop to the top of the water and begin to skim across it. This is not necessarily good. As you continue to skim across the water, your legs will almost invariably begin to separate and simply continue to do so until at last you'll feel much like the wishbone of a Thanksgiving turkey in the process of being sundered. At this juncture, you'll probably wish you could fall. Some evil force, however, will prevent this and your legs will simply become increasingly splayed, while you scream your head off. Unaccountably, those in the boat will take this as a signal to go faster. And, if you continue to fail to fall, you will cross the boat's wake, and reach a speed normally achieved only in a cyclotron. When you do fall–and don't delude yourself, you will–you will have come to a much greater appreciation of what the term "hard water" actually means.

SCUBA DIVING

The only unquestioned pleasures in scuba diving are that when you're fully immersed in water no one can sell you insurance, serve you with a summons or try to convince you to become a Jehovah's witness. Besides these benefits, scuba diving can best be compared to taking a bath while bound in enormous rubber bands. As if that weren't bad enough, there are, moreover, a number of horrifying things to keep in mind. One thing to remember is that even if you obey all the rules, follow every procedure and say your prayers every night before bed, there's still the possibility that your blood will boil and your ear drums will burst. In brief, you're a lot more likely to experience "Rapture of the Deep" than you are any deep sense of rapture, so why go? Also remember that, with the possible exception of Rex Reed, sea snakes are the most venomous creatures known to humankind. Furthermore, when sexually aroused, sea snakes are very aggressive and likely to bite you. (The same may be true of Mr. Reed, of course. I don't know.) Furthermore, when scuba diving, you will look even more like a basking seal than you do when water skiing. Need I remind you that basking seals are what sharks eat?! Finally remember that no matter how long you're under water or how deep you go, all you're really going to see are fish and clams; no matter what Jacques Cousteau says, fish and clams are every bit as stupid looking underwater as they are on land.

FUN IN THE SKY

Possibly one thing is more unnatural to humans than being underwater and that's going up in the air. In my opinion, anybody who would do anything more than ten feet off the ground without a flight crew and someone serving drinks to calm the nerves, deserves an immediate and rather thorough psychological examination. Let's start with bungee jumpers. Is anyone unwilling to question the sanity of someone who dives hundreds of feet backwards off a bridge? And for what?! Where's the fun? One can only presume that it's the sheer thrill of survival. If this is fun, what's Russian roulette? And what about sky diving? It simply isn't normal to jump out of an airplane, at least not without the urgent prodding of a bayonette-bearing superior officer at your back. Again, where's the pleasure? There you are plummeting towards the earth, subject to the whimsical winds, a mere pawn of gravity. In the event of a failed rip cord or an improperly packed chute, you will end your life in a condition which will permit a burial in a standard size-ten envelope. Isn't there something else you can do on a Saturday morning?

Finally, let us consider hang gliding. In this activity, you will depend on the flimsiest, most rudimentary and childish of all aircrafts, the kite. Recall what happened to the kites you flew as a child. Routinely, they became entangled in electrical wires. Invariably, they crashed into trees and were shredded by the force of the impact. Time after time, they spun uncontrollably towards the earth despite your frantic efforts to keep them aloft. So why are you betting your life on one? Let us also remember that hang glider manufacturers are constantly announcing design improvements. Don't you find it disconcerting to know that this thing you're sailing around on hundreds of feet up in the sky needs to be improved? Suppose the inevitable happens and you get hit by an unanticipated downdraft, updraft or side shear and begin to plunge, twirling out of control towards a premature reunion with earth. What's going to protect you? Your helmet? Besides which, if you truly want to feel like a bird, might I suggest you simply sit on an egg and leave it at that?

GOING TO SPORTS EVENTS

One of my earliest memories is of almost being crushed by a fat man with three fingers who was trying to push himself into a ticket line ahead of my grandmother and myself at a Philadelphia Phillies baseball game. This pattern of rude and boorish behavior has been repeated at just about every sports event I've ever attended. Invariably, we are exposed to hordes of rampaging geeks. They drink, scream and shove. If their mothers ever saw them acting this way, most males at a sports event would be immediately sent to bed. Frequently sociologists try to figure out what makes people–from the inebriated nitwits baring their chests in sub-zero weather at Monday night football games to the brutal bashers squashing their fellow fans at international soccer events–behave this way. The answer is simple. They're jerks. They're jerks at home, at work and at sporting events; they're jerks without restraint.

Thus, they curse, shove and fight. Is this fun? Is this what you want to expose your kids to? And this doesn't even take into consideration the fact that you'll have to buy hot dogs at ten times the normal price, use a bathroom that hasn't been cleaned since it was built and sit in a seat that's far enough from the field that the athletes will look like microbes.

BASEBALL

Baseball still claims to be America's national pastime. Of course, hearing this is rather like hearing an eighty-year-old woman tell you she's still beautiful: it's probably not true but what's the point in objecting? Let's face it, most American's would rather go see a bunch of lunkheads bash their heads in and tear their ligaments up while playing football. Anyway, at a baseball game what you usually get to see is, well, nothing. At least nothing other than guys spitting tobacco juice in the dust and fiddling with their clothes in their crotch areas. (What is it with baseball players and their groins? Are they so special, and so different that they really require all this constant attention and adjusting? Or are these guys more or less just playing with themselves in public?) In truth, the only good thing about baseball is that it lets you spend a hot summer afternoon hardly moving. In fact, a spectator can generally ignore a baseball game for hours at a time and still not miss much; despite all the frenzied malarkey written about the subtleties, intricacies, and (oh, please!) elegance of the game, is why vast numbers of Americans still bother to go. Next to watching TV, going to a baseball game is about as close as you can come to America's true passion, total inertia.

FOOTBALL

Everybody knows that most women don't understand football and kind of hate it at the same time, and maybe they're right. After all, the experience of watching a football game consists largely of watching hordes of men stand around with brief lapses into brutality. This is something you could also experience by going to a busy intersection and waiting for a thirty car pileup. Besides, if football games are so interesting to watch, how do you explain the invention of "the wave"?

BASKETBALL

Unlike football, a lot of women like basketball. This may be because they get to look at very tall guys in very short pants; it's sort of a stretch version of the Chippendales. Basketball games are also one of few opportunities black and white people ever get to be on the same side of any issue in this society. This is rare and worthy of cheering for. In fact, I only have two minor complaints about basketball. One, of course, is Bill Lambier. The other is that one of the primary skills is called "dribbling." I mean, couldn't they have thought of something a little more, I don't know, mature?

HOCKEY

What exactly is the appeal of an activity during which the high point is when somebody loses a tooth, gets jabbed in the eye with a stick or receives stiches without an anesthetic? And when hockey isn't brutal, it's boring. The puck slides this way, the puck slides that way. Figures dressed in enough equipment to withstand a direct nuclear attack push each other into walls. Let's be frank, the real reason there are so many fights in the NHL is because the game's so fundamentally dull, fights are the only way to keep people interested. Let's also remember that hockey has traditionally been played and enjoyed by Canadians who have almost nothing else to talk about and will do almost anything to try to keep warm.

Vacations:
You Can Get Away from It All, but Never Far Enough

EUROPEAN VACATIONS

*"Vacations are anticipated with great joy and
remembered with great nostalgia but experienced
with great difficulty."*

Anonymous

Frequently the pursuit of fun is nothing more than a search for changed circumstances in which we trade one form of pain for another while deluding ourselves that this new agony will somehow be preferable to the old one. We call this a vacation. Indeed, it is only the hope that life elsewhere won't be the same muddled puddle of boredom we experience at home that could possibly induce us to pack our bags, leave our homes and risk spending several hours on an airplane seated next to a French person. Yet, despite our great expectations, we inevitably return from some far-flung, filthy corner of the earth irritated, enervated and nearly bankrupt. Invariably we express some sadder but wiser sentiment such as "after a vacation like that, I could use a vacation!" Or the well-worn, "there's no place like home!"

Memory is misleading, however, and travel agents are indefatigable, so sooner or later we find ourselves once again wandering through the musty castles of Wales, contending with the acid waiters of France or screaming pointless obscenities into an inoperative Italian telephone. You see, while every trip begins with the hope of discovering something wonderful, it invariably ends with the discovery that people are the same disagreeable species no matter where you go. So while travel may be broadening, it's hardly ever fun.

FRANCE

It never takes the French long to make it clear that they don't like you. Don't take this personally, however, because they don't like each other much either. Their incessant sense of distaste helps explain why the French have turned sneering into something of a national pastime. If you don't speak their language, for instance, the French will sneer at your ignorance. If you do speak their language, they will sneer at your accent. In France there's just no way to avoid getting sneered at unless you keep looking up. Another thing the French will make clear is that they have culture and you don't. Given the fact that their culture includes urinating on public sidewalks, one has to wonder why they're the ones who are sneering. At any rate, if you go to France, don't bring your good shoes, and watch where you walk.

GREAT BRITAIN

Britain is beautiful, not to mention full of historic wonders, and you may even enjoy it if don't stay there long enough to eat. Unquestionably the best thing you can get to eat there is beer. In Ireland there's a passion for the potato which can only be accounted for by tasting the rest of their food. In Scotland they will try to feed you a traditional dish cum local joke known as haggis, which will give you the odd sensation of consuming a bag of wet sand. One thing you will notice almost everywhere in Great Britain is that the people have bad teeth. That's because in Britain there's no point in having good teeth. You'd only have to eat more.

ITALY

There are two types of Italian men: those who grow tomatoes and those who want to sleep with them. Keep this in mind and you'll know what to expect on a trip to Italy. The food will be great if you like tomato sauce, but if you're a female, you may expect to get chased down the street by Italian men who will pinch your buttocks until you're black and blue. (Of course, if you're a child you can expect Italian women to pinch your cheeks until they're black and blue, and if you're a vegetable, you can expect to be pinched by everyone. You see, to Italians, pinching is what sneering is to the French–sort of an unofficial, national pastime.) At any rate, if you go to Rome you can expect to get caught in a traffic jam, which will last from approximately the time you get there until the time you go home. If you travel in southern Italy, you'll just have to watch out for the banditos along the road. And if you stay in northern Italy you may, at times, think you're in Germany. This is not a pleasant thought.

GERMANY

We've all heard about the German problem, which is largely that Germans are born without a sense of humor. Absolutely nein. So don't bother translating your jokes. The Germans won't understand them and, even if they do, they won't laugh. Thus, the main thing to fear from German reunification is not the increased military strength but rather the huge humor vacuum which will result in Central Europe. This could lead to a frightening wit imbalance and, before you know it, the middle of the continent could once again become the grim, grey, dull region it was under communism.

FINLAND

In summer the midnight sun will keep you up long past your bedtime. In winter you run the risk of becoming freeze-dried while being beaten with birch rods. This is called taking a sauna. No wonder the suicide rate is one of the world's highest. In Finland dying is the way to have fun.

IRELAND

There are only two things you can do in Ireland; get drunk or get shot. So, why not go to Detroit?

ICELAND

Don't you think maybe the name's a clue? I mean, why would anybody go to a place called Iceland. If you do go, don't pack your bikini.

USSR

Russia is now trying to attract western tourists. Once you get there, you'll find the only place serving food is McDonald's. Is this really worth the trip?

SPAIN

Bullfights are the biggest tourist attraction in Spain. Basically, they are akin to watching someone in stretch pants work at a meat packing plant. Seriously, once the parade's over and the music stops, you more or less just sit there and watch a cow get tortured to death. This is your idea of fun?

GREECE

Twenty-five hundred years ago the Greeks had a great civilization. But, frankly, what have they done lately? Souvlaki is not enough. In 2,500 years you'd think they could have come up with wine that didn't taste like asphalt. Give the place a pass, and I don't mean at Thermopylae.

SEEING AMERICA'S WORST: DRIVING CROSS-COUNTRY WITH YOUR FAMILY

There are basically two ways to see the United States with your family. But the horrors of flying are so well-documented, I needn't go into them. Indeed not even the airline industry pretends that flying on a commercial airline is truly fun. Everyone knows you can lose your life as well as your luggage, and even if you make it alive, you'll still have to spend hours in a seat which has clearly been designed for something much smaller than a human, maybe a rhesus monkey.

However, flying is at least fast. The same cannot be said for driving across America, particularly with a car full of children. While there are certain automobile clubs and gasoline industry associations which will try to tell you that crossing this great continent with a car full of kids can be enjoyable, anybody who has ever done it agrees that it's the closest you can come to dental torture, without actually opening your mouth. Here's what happens.

Within an hour of leaving the house, your buttocks will be sore. Within two hours, your kids will begin singing "99 Bottles of Beer on the Wall." They will continue singing this song for the duration of your trip, an act that in many states is considered a full and sufficient defense in cases of justifiable homicide. Within three hours, your back will hurt and your head will ache. Within four hours, your children will begin an argument that will last until you get home. By the end of the first day, your kids will plead with you to stop every time you pass an ice cream stand or a motel with a swimming pool and color television. They will sulk if you don't. If you do stop, they will insist that you buy something you would never consider buying if you were at home and not subjected to the peculiar

80

dementia of travel. By the end of this day, you will earnestly wish you'd never heard of America, let alone embarked on an effort to cross it. By the end of the trip, you will silently swear to yourself that next time you will take an airplane. Even if you crash, at least it wouldn't take so long.

AND WHEN YOU GET THERE

Here's what you can expect to see at some of America's most memorable sites.

THE GRAND CANYON–The world's longest, biggest and deepest ditch.

CARLSBAD CAVERNS–This may well be the high point of your trip. When the guide turns off the lights to demonstrate how no light can enter the cave, you will not be able to see the other members of your family for the first time in weeks. You will cherish this moment and wish it could last.

BIG SUR–Big trees. Big deal.

THE PAINTED DESERT–Unfortunately it's all painted the same color red.

NIAGARA FALLS–A huge jacuzzi.

LAS VEGAS–In this city you'll come to understand that "fun" is not just a word people use when they're trying to sell you something; it's a word they also use when they're trying to rob you. Anyone not bored to a state near death might wonder exactly what the fun is in putting your money in a machine and watching it disappear. Or exactly how you derive pleasure from putting your life savings on a table and watching somebody else pick it up? Presumably, this phenomenon can only be explained by people who consider "Shecky" a legitimate name.

MIAMI–This city used to remind people of Israel because it was warm, sunny and had a large Jewish population. Now it reminds people of Israel because of the extraordinary likelihood that you'll get shot.

ST. LOUIS–The city's main attraction, the Gateway to the West, looks like one half of the world's largest McDonald's sign. Isn't this a good reason to stay where you are?

BOSTON–It's like New York without the good parts.

NEW ORLEANS–During Mardi Gras you will be forced to wonder whether this is really a city or just some vast work release program from a nearby mental hospital.

PHILADELPHIA–W.C. Fields was right.

CALIFORNIA–The main reason not to go to California isn't the constant threat of mud slides, fire storms or "the Big One"–it's the populace. Californians, you see, long ago replaced Texans as the group of people most likely to make a big deal out of where they live. (By Californians, of course, I mean Southern Californians. Northern Californians are just misplaced and slightly drier Oregonians.) Californians are also the most aggressive about letting you know how much fun they're having and will invariably insist that you join them. Usually what they want you to join them in is some form of behavior that's better left to juveniles such as surf boarding, hang gliding, what have you. Oddly enough, while enamored of fun, native Californians are rarely funny. Funny Californians come from somewhere else, like Brooklyn. In fact, compared to a native Californian, even Germans are a riot. However, as those choirboys of coastal *joie de vivre*, the Beach Boys demonstrate, no one has suffered more from their desperate pursuit of fun than Californians themselves. Despite having written a virtual anthem to fun, one member is a mad recluse. Another is dead from drug abuse. And the rest have become pitiable examples of perpetually arrested adolescence. This is fun? No wonder Daddy took the T-Bird away.

WASHINGTON–Ironically, the capital of this country is now virtually indistinguishable from the capitals of most third world countries: masses of poverty-stricken people live in substandard housing through which an army of arrogant, pinstriped bureaucrats passes in chauffeur-driven Mercedes. Makes you proud to be an American.

NEW YORK CITY–Is there any more irrefutable evidence of what a fraud this notion of fun is than the fact that New York once actually had the nerve to call itself "Fun City"?! Seriously, for decades, New York had a well-earned reputation for being a behavioral sinkpit where greedy sociopaths were in open competition with the criminally insane to see who could get to your pocketbook first. Then all of a sudden it became "Fun City"?! Come on, now! I mean, New York may be a lot of things. It may be the mighty citadel of commerce and the center of all that is magnificent, but I doubt whether it's even a semi-normal person's idea of fun. Besides, if you can make it here, you can make it anywhere. So why not just stay home?

FUN IN THE SUN

If you live in a cold climate, winter is the time of year when your thoughts most frequently turn to murder, suicide or visiting someplace warm. For two months you'll endure life with a nose that's comically red and painfully raw, feet that are incessantly damp and lungs that ache from persistent hacking. Finally, you will decide to go someplace that's sunny, warm and exotic. For several bleak weeks, the mere thought of this upcoming tropical idyll will nourish and sustain you. And then you'll get there, although your luggage probably won't. You will find sand in your bed, food that's impossible to eat and natives who hate you. In the process of acquiring a tan, your neck will become blistered, and your knee joints will become crisped to the point where even the simple act of walking will be an unendurable agony. This won't be the worst of it, though. Within two days you will also have some sort of gastrointestinal problem. You will either find yourself (a) utterly incapable of eliminating, or (b) capable of eliminating once every twenty seconds. Should you somehow escape these eventualities, there is still every chance in the world that you will step on a sea urchin or cut your foot on coral. Please remember that coral is not some benign, little plant; it's a form of animal life that can grow inside your circulatory system and turn you into some sort of human trinket.

In any event, if it's hot and sunny, the only memento you will have of this trip is a picture of yourself grimacing from the pain of your sunburn while wearing a bathing suit you'd be embarrassed to be seen in anywhere else. On the other hand, if the weather's rainy, dank and dismal, you will be forced to stay in a musty, motel room constantly calculating the extraordinary amount of money you're paying to be miserable. Have fun.

CRUISE SHIPS

*"Being on a ship is like being in jail, except a
man in jail has more room, better food and
commonly better company."*

Samuel Johnson

Perhaps the most telling observation about cruise liners is that the advertisements for one company now call their vessels "fun ships." This is, of course, a transparent effort to combat the notion, held from time immemorial, quite accurately, that cruise ships are little more than sumptuous, floating prisons. In fact, there's almost nothing to do on a cruise ship but play shuffleboard, stare into the sunset and eat until you require radical liposuction. The truth is you might enjoy being on a cruise ship if you think you might also enjoy being a Strasbourgh goose; an animal that has its feet nailed to the floor and is force-fed until it's liver becomes inflamed and can be made into pâté.

In an effort to conceal the immutable dullness of shipboard life, cruise ship companies have created an entire subspecies of professional fun-mongers known as cruise directors. On board, cruise directors have but a single mission, which is to distract you by any means possible from the fact that you haven't done much more than sit in a deck chair, stare at the sun and shovel food in your face since you checked into your stateroom. Thus, when you're lying on a deck chair, trying to let your latest ingurgitation pass, a cruise director will pick you up and push you into a jacuzzi. When you're waddling about the foredeck, blind with the pain of indigestion, a cruise director will grab you by the elbow and shove you in the direction of a shuffleboard court. When you're leaning over the ship's rail, humming loudly to mask the sound of roiling borborygmus, a cruise director will guide you by the hand in an effort to make you dance with someone you'd prefer not to touch. In short, cruise directors operate on the same principle as the mothers of three-year-olds; you can't be happy and they can't rest unless you're doing something they construe as fun. Worse yet, there's no escape. If you open your mouth in complain, a cruise dirctor will simply shove food in it. The only comforting thought is that it's hard to imagine any country that would actually prosecute you for strangling a cruise director.

Sooner or later, however, your cruise will come to an end and friends and relatives will come to greet you. "How was it?" they will ask. "The food," you will exclaim, "you wouldn't believe the food!" The fact is, however, they will find it easy to believe anything you tell them about the food, since it will be painfully obvious you've recently consumed more than the populations of some third world countries. The only thing they won't be able to believe is that you spent the last two weeks on a cruise liner and not at an all-you-can-eat restaurant.

THE BEACH

When the weather's hot and the water's warm, you will probably decide to go to the beach. Of course, so will everyone else in the world. Thus, you'll typically encounter the first major nuisance of the day approximately at the end of your driveway, which is the traffic jam leading to the beach. For many angry hours, this traffic jam will be your life. As you creep along, with tempers flaring, gasoline burning and family fuming, it will give you an excellent idea of what purgatory might be like. Eventually, you will reach the beach. Of course, so will everybody else in the world. The scene will be reminiscent of downtown Hong Kong in spandex. In searching for a few square feet of sand to call your own, you will wend your way through greased bodies lying in tormented positions. At last you will find a spot of beach large enough to accommodate your towel. Unfamiliar families with squalling children will be mere inches from your toes. Beer-swilling swine will be perched near your ear. Arrogant adolescents will throw footballs, baseballs, volleyballs, frisbees and jarts without apparent concern for your safety or location. The only thing louder than the ocean's roar will be the boom boxes which surround you. And you were planning to read? Sooner or later, in the midst of acquiring a vicious sunburn, you will become hot and sweaty. Presuming there's no riptide, undertow or shark alert, you can go in the water to cool off. Of course, you could have also cooled off by staying home and turning on the air conditioner. So why didn't you? Besides, how much fun is swimming anyway? You will get water up your nose and in your ears. If you swim near a child, you are merely accepting an invitation to bathe in his urine. At any rate, you are still moving through an element the creator intended for crabs, fish and whales. Ultimately, you will emerge from the brine with the ruby eyes of an enraged frog.

After a few hours of this fun, you will pick up your blanket and walk to your car. You and everybody else. Once seated in your car, you will discover you have sand in your bathing suit. How are you going to get it out now? You will be hot, sticky and tired. You will be stuck in a traffic jam all the way home.

TOURING AN HISTORICAL PLACE

Once in a lifetime, many parents make the mistake of trying to acquaint their children with the history of this nation by taking them to a historically significant city or village. On this trip parents learn that if there is one thing their children are not interested in, it's American history. What children are interested in is Disney World. Indeed throughout any trip to an historic site, your children will seem to have taken an oath of silence. They will remain glumly and sullenly mute. Typically they will speak only to ask (a) why you didn't go to Disney World this year (b) if you can go to Disney World next year, or (c) when you're going home. As for yourself, you will discover many things, none of them interesting. If you go to Plymouth Rock, for instance, you will discover that it may be famous, but it's still just a rock. Similarly, if you go to a famous battlefield, you will discover that it looks exactly like any other field, except with a souvenir shop and a place that charges an admission fee. Meanwhile, here's what will happen.

The first time you go through a famous, historical house, you will discover that your historical tour guide has the uncanny capacity to make you drowsy within a single, spoken sentence. This experience will be repeated at each famous, historical house you tour. By the time you tour your third, historical house, your children will look like they are on a death march.

Once inside a famous, historical house, you will be told where the famous, historical person who lived there ate, worked and slept. There is, however, only one thing your children will ever be interested in: where the famous, historical person went to the bathroom.

When you go to a restaurant, you will be greeted and served by people in silly hats. Males will wear silly, three-cornered hats, females will wear hats that look like toaster covers. For your children, making fun of these hats will be the high point of the trip. In most of these places, you will get menus with s's that look like f's. Your children will spend three quarters of an hour arguing about whether these letters are really f's or s's. Finally, they will order Belgian waffles anyway.

After you've toured far too many famous historical sites and homes, you will be forced to browse through row upon row of "shoppes." Just as a sick animal knows it must wander and suffer until, at last, it can find a place to die, you will instinctively understand that the rest of the day will be spent going from shoppe to shoppe to shoppe accumulating a collection of junk you would never buy at home.

Finally, you will visit the Village Gaol. Your kids will spend three quarters of an hour arguing about the pronunciation of the word "gaol" and then ask you to take photos of them locked in the wooden stocks. You will probably wish you could leave them there. You will, however, have learned a profoundly, important lesson: if you're going to have a rendezvous with history, don't take the kids.

TAKING THE FAMILY
TO A THEME PARK

As a parent, sooner or later, you will get the feeling your kids are growing up too fast and you're not sharing enough special experiences with them. This is a notion your kids will do nothing to dispel, knowing that every time they see a certain wistful look in your eyes, they can expect to receive a doll or a baseball mitt. This is also a notion the people at Walt Disney and the American travel industry will do nothing to dispel. Inevitably, you will be exposed to a TV commercial which will show you what a really happy American family does, which is not just sit around the house and watch television, but rather travel to a theme park with the kids. Once your kids have seen this TV commercial featuring droves of tickled tots partaking of every known, childish pleasure, they will begin an incessant chorus. "We wanna go. We wanna go. We wanna go," they will greet you in the morning. "We wanna go. We wanna go. We wanna go," they will drone during the day. "We wanna go. We wanna go. We wanna go," they will drowsily chant while slouching off to bed. Relentlessly, with ever-mounting fury, the chorus will continue until finally, a pathetic husk of your former self will capitulate, "All right, for Christ's sake, we'll go!" Your kids will celebrate, "Yeeehhh, this'll be great!"

Once at the theme park, you will find that, as promised, you are indeed much closer together than you had originally thought and not just with your own family, but with most families in America. You will, in fact, be surrounded by approximately two billion other families who have all succumbed to precisely the same sales pitch. Consequently, from the time you arrive until the time you leave, you will do little more than stand in one interminable line after another. You will stand in line to get into the place. You will stand in line to get tickets for each exhibit and ride. You will stand in line to go to the bathroom. To get on a ride or in an exhibit, you will stand in lines with no apparent beginning or end. Assaulted by the insidious clink of one cash register after another, you and your family will stumble about with numbed indifference, bickering incessantly, as eager to leave as you were to come.

When your family announces its hunger–which it will do with expensive regularity–you will stand in one line to get soda and pizza, another for hot dogs and beer and yet a third line for dessert. Perhaps you will have a dim memory of having seen food lines like this someplace before. Perhaps in a sepia tone photo of people in Ireland during the Potato Famine or in a documentary about the bread lines during the Great Depression. No where else in contemporary America, however, will you have ever encountered lines this long composed of people with an urgent need to eat.

Sadly, when you get to the end of these lines, being jostled all the while by people with the coarse habits of camel herders and assailed by indefatigably irritating teenagers dressed in costume, you will make a horrifying discovery: a theme park is nothing more than an amusement park with higher prices and a roving band of nincompoops pretending to be cartoon characters. The only magic in this kingdom is how they manage to keep people coming back.

Momma Said There'd Be Days Like This, but She Never Went into Detail

NEW YEAR'S EVE

"May old acquaintance be forgot."

Robert Burns

New Year's Eve begins with four days of warnings about traffic fatalities and ends with a splitting headache. In between, there is much noise and little joy. All in all, it provides the most conclusive evidence that fun is almost invariably loathsome. Despite our certain knowledge of how this gruesome ritual will proceed year after year we seem constrained to celebrate the occasion.

While sadly there seems to be no way to avoid acknowledging this holiday, there are basically only three ways to spend it. You can stay home alone, all by yourself, and quietly endure the ordeal while watching several thousand nitwits cheer the falling of a ball in Times Square. If you do this, however, you will unquestionably suffer some kind of anxiety and depression. After all, what kind of loser doesn't get invited anywhere on New Year's Eve? On the other hand, you may decide to celebrate the evening with a few close friends. If you do this, you run the greater risk that the evening will evolve into an acrimonious exchange of bitter truths reminiscent of the revelations of George and Martha in *Who's Afraid of Virgina Woolf?* After all, it's an evening during which we're encouraged to reflect on all that's gone before and frequently all that's gone before leads to an argument. Last, you can go to a big New Year's Eve bash which will probably be given by someone you barely know and attended by people you don't really like. Much like any tragedy, it will proceed with a certain inevitability. During the early evening, you will drink too much. At the stroke of midnight, someone you've been avoiding all night will throw confetti in your face, blow a noisemaker in your ear and try to ram his tongue down your throat. By one o'clock in the morning, you will have become entirely numb and will have passed out on top of the coats in the bedroom. By three o'clock in the morning, you will have thrown up twice and torn the seat off a toilet. By five o'clock in the morning, you will have regained feeling in most parts of your body, but wish you hadn't. By six o'clock in the morning, strange noises not unlike those our Civil Defense System employs to alert people to an imminent attack will be issued from deep inside your head. By seven o'clock in the morning, you will ardently wish you were attached to a life-support system, so you could simply unplug it and die. Sometime during that day, as an act of insincere contrition, you will make a resolution to never drink, smoke or attend a New Year's Eve party again. You will wait one year and repeat the entire evening's events.

ST. PATRICK'S DAY

To my mind, the ultimate proof of the lunacy of the race from which I claim partial descent is not in its documented tendency to get drunk, in its indisputable record of public rowdiness or in its unaccountable passion for the potato, but rather the fact that the Irish have chosen what is the most awful time of year on which to celebrate their own, special holiday.

Invariably on St. Patrick's Day, it will start to rain then change to snow. Presumabl, this would be tolerable if it weren't for the fact that, while standing exposed to the horrid elements, one is required to watch corpulent hordes of florid-faced policeman play one rancid rendition after another of "Danny Boy," "MacNarmara's Band" and "Who Put the Overalls in Mrs. Murphy's Chowder?" While it has never been established with any certainty just why the snakes left Ireland, I think the fact of the matter may be that snakes are simply music lovers and the music played by Irish police gave them no reason to stay. On the other hand, of course, snakes are reputed to be deaf, so perhaps it wasn't the music that drove them away after all. Maybe it was that obnoxious color one is forced to wear. Lacking the ability to hear, one may reasonably suppose that snakes are visually sensitive creatures who found that dressing up in something the color of a Key Lime pie, even for a single day, was more than they could bear. Many humans, of course, feel the same way. Indeed, if it were not for the fear of being beaten senseless by someone with red hair and freckles or the equally intimidating threat of hearing an endless harangue on the incessant squabbles in Irish history, do you really suppose most people would choose to put on socks, pants or anything else the color of kryptonite? Do you really imagine that we'd elect to drink bright green beer, chomp on bright green potato chips or chew on bright green corned-beef sandwiches? Of course, not. We're simply bullied into it by people whose idea of a good time is to stand in the rain and listen to bad music. No wonder the snakes left. They were probably glad to go.

JULY FOURTH

Independence Day represents the fulfillment of many of the noblest aspirations and most dearly held dreams of humankind. It's a day on which our forefathers proclaimed the rule of law and the supremacy of reason while establishing a free and democratic nation where we could live together with our fellow citizens in harmony and peace. This is, in short, what America's all about.

So, how do we celebrate the occasion? Weeks in advance we cross state lines to purchase illegal fireworks. We then casually distribute these fireworks amongst our children so they can lob them at neighbors, toss them to friends and hurl them at pets. On the day in question, we greet the morning by drinking the first of perhaps a dozen cans of beer, knowing full well that by the end of the day, we have every intention of driving drunk. So much for the Rule of Law.

In the afternoon, we go to parades and cheer with jingoistic malice while troops, tanks, Boy Scouts and fire trucks lumber past us. At dusk we drive to public parks where it's impossible to find a parking place and form an irritable horde with our bibulous fellow citizens. We spread blankets. We open coolers. We argue over who was here first, who's in whose way and who's encroaching on whose square yard of claimed turf. So much for peace and harmony.

At the culmination of the day's events we watch concussive bombs explode in the sky. We ooh and ahh. We expound on the beauties of burning gunpowder, to tots who are hiding their heads. We remark on the magnificent thunder, to kids who are holding their ears. At last, it's time to go. We leave mounds of empty beer cans, ripped potato chip bags, half-eaten sandwiches and plastic bags where we sat and then drive home with an illegal alcohol level in our blood streams. This is what our country's all about?

THANKSGIVING

At Thanksgiving one is forced to suspect that the real turkey is not on the table. The real turkey is the one preparing the meal. You see, despite the name, this has always been an occasion of consummate thanklessness for anyone who spends any time fixing dinner. Originally, this was the Indians. Our Pilgrim ancestors thanked them for the lavish feast, and for rescuing them from starvation by taking their land and extirpating them from the face of the earth. The tradition continues.

These days, it's usually grannies and moms who suffer our ingratitude. For days in advance they're confined to the kitchen making relishes, sauces and pies. On Thanksgiving Day itself, they toil and moil in the kitchen, sweating like pigs, preparing the bird. (And it better be turkey that they're making, with mashed potatoes, cranberry sauce and whatever else the crowd expects. New recipes are not appreciated on Thanksgiving. It's all part of the whole, ungrateful tradition.) Finally the food is set on the table. After a hastily muttered, insincere prayer, the meal is gobbled by ungrateful relatives with barely more than a few grunts, random belches and various commands to "pass the potatoes" in the way of thanks. In short, Thanksgiving is to humans what feeding frenzies are to piranhas: a great chance to eat a lot without having to worry about your waistline.

At any rate, within minutes after completion of the meal, all males in attendance will be on their way into the living room to watch the first of approximately a dozen football games. Within half an hour after that, all male relatives will be asleep and will remain so until the kitchen is clean, the dishes are done and everything's been put away. At this precise moment, as though summoned by some unheard command, all male relatives will rise, stumble towards the kitchen and make turkey sandwiches while covering every available surface with cranberry sauce, mayonnaise, giblet gravy and little bits of stuffing. They will then return to the sofa and resume slumbering and/or watching the TV. This process will continue until there are simply no more football games to watch. At this point all attending males will stand, stretch, yawn, threaten to return at Christmas and leave. Some thanks.

CHRISTMAS

Many of us celebrate Christmas with a family fruitcake. All of us, however, celebrate Christmas with a fruitcake family. The simple truth is that during the holidays, you will have to spend more time with your relatives than is humanly endurable. You'll have to send cards to people whose names you can barely remember, exchange gifts with people you've never liked, visit people you'll spend the rest of the year avoiding, and eat a lot of food you can't stand. In the process, you'll gain fifty pounds you can't afford.

If you're married, you'll spend the entire time before Christmas arguing with your spouse. You will argue about things such as how to decorate the house and whether to get a tree. One of you will insist that Christmas "just wouldn't be Christmas without decorations and a tree." This is, of course, correct. It would be much more relaxing.

If you're a kid, things are even worse. In the hope that you will get something you actually want, you will have to spend the entire time between Thanksgiving and Christmas letting repulsive relatives kiss you on the lips. Ugh! You'll have to sit on the lap of a strange old man who's masquerading as Santa Claus, and reveal your innermost thoughts and desires. Ick! You'll have to write a letter to the North Pole that will never get sent. Finally you'll give your parents a list that will be ignored.

You see, despite all your efforts, on Christmas morning you will typically receive gifts that will seem to have been bought for someone else—someone who is much older than you. You will get underwear, socks, pajamas, clip-on ties, shirts with epaulettes, cologne and mother-of-pearl cuff links. Even the gifts that bear some similarity to the ones you asked for, still won't really be right. You will always get the wrong model, the wrong brand or the wrong size. Never ever, will you get those carefully considered items you requested. As you open box after disappointing box, a small, shrill voice will start to shriek inside you. What's the matter with your parents? Didn't they read your meticulously compiled list? Didn't they pay the least attention to the commercials you exhorted them to watch? Were they deliberately indifferent to the unequivocal hints you dropped? Or did they, perhaps, get some other child's Christmas list by mistake? Perhaps the list of a violin prodigy who might actually need mother-of-pearl cuff links? Desperately you will calculate the number of days until your birthday when, once again, you can ask for for what you really want. This will be one of the first, strong intimations you will have that it will never really matter what you say to your parents because they will never listen to you anyway. Happy Holidays.

I HATE A PARADE

The only two people who indisputably love a parade are the drum major and the baton twirler. The former because it's one of the few occasions on which a cross-dresser can prance in public without being accused of deviant behavior. The latter because it's the only place a girl with thighs the size of a beffalo can garner any sort of public admiration at all. The remainder of the band will look like an ambulatory casting call for *The Ballad of the Sad Cafe*. So why are you watching them?

In any case, being in a parade is pretty much a waste of time, and watching one is nothing more than an advanced form of loitering. Either way, there are two things you know for sure: (a) by the time it's over your feet will hurt, and (b) you're going to hear a lot of bad music. Seriously, if the musicians were good, wouldn't they be in orchestras where they could sit down and be comfortable, instead of walking around outside exposing themselves to both the elements and public ridicule? And even in those rare cases when the musicians are good, what about the music? Why, in fact, was the second piece of marching band music ever written? Wasn't one enough? With the possible exception of the descendants of John Phillip Sousa, who can even tell the difference between the first piece of marching band music and the second?

There is one thing at a parade, however, that is normally even more unpalatable than the music. The food. You'll find that the chestnuts are burnt on the outside and have the consistency of a brain tumor on the inside. Cold hot dogs will be fished from oily water and laid to rest on week-old buns. Hard, stale pretzels will be handed to you by a man who has, without question, recently used his fingers to clean his ears. And cotton candy which, aside from its extraordinary capacity to wind up in children's hair, amounts to nothing more than extremely expensive, flavored air.

Finally, let us consider the intrinsic interest of the parades themselves. I mean, what are you really watching? At the Rose Bowl Parade, you're watching a procession of mobile flower arrangements that was originally conceived of by Pasadena real estate salesmen, in order to sell desert land to suckers from the East. At the Macy's Day Parade, you're being asked to follow big, dumb balloons to a department store. In either case, you're being commercially exploited in a way that borders on the laughable. Does this make you feel smart? Let us quit this subject with the most intriguing question of all: if you can never find a cop when you want one, how come there are always thousands of them in parades?

BIRTHDAYS: ANOTHER YEAR OLDER AND DEEPER IN DEBT

When you're a kid your peers will spend your birthday tirelessly punching you on the arm, once for each year of your life. This is a mere harbinger of things to come and the first premonition you will have that, despite the ice cream, cake, candy, hats and gifts, your birthday is really only an occasion for abusing you.

In your youth, of course, the abuse will take the simple, direct, physical form mentioned above. As you get older, however, the abuse becomes increasingly psychological. As you reach twenty-five or thirty years of age, for instance, your birthday will be an occasion for people to make remarks, oozing with barely veiled hostility, about how many wrinkles you have and how much longer you can expect to have enough hair to make it worth combing. By the time you're forty years old, people will start saying things like, "Gee, you really look good....for 40!" The implication being that you're lucky to be strolling around without a walker. At this time you will also start to receive gifts such as large bottles of cologne, which will probably be around a lot longer than you will. Depressing. You will also be forced to wear a silly party hat, eat ice cream and cake and generally be treated like a seven-year-old. This is no mistake. It's a deliberate reference to the fact that your second childhood is impending.

The kiss of death, though, is when they start putting a single candle on your cake, clearly intimating that your lungs aren't powerful enough to extinguish the number of candles equal to the number of your years. At this point a birthday party is little more than a practice funeral, and you shouldn't be overly surprised if people start telling you that you look "very life-like" and that, for all your faults, you were really a nice person deep down inside.

Of all the forms of irritation meted out on your birthday, however, perhaps the worst is the ritual singing of the most graceless, unpleasant and unimaginative tune ever written, "Happy Birthday." No one enjoys hearing it and only obnoxious, young boys who see it as an opportunity to exercise their wit by singing sophomoric lyrics, enjoy singing it. Finally, there's the most loathsome of all pranks, the surprise party. Having reached a certain age, you will come home desiring nothing more than the chance to kick off your shoes, loosen your girdle and, perhaps, remove your false teeth. Suddenly you will be ambushed by people you know but do not necessarily wish to see. Inevitably, you will be forced to use your false teeth and grin at those people as though you are somehow delighted by the prospect of being another year older and closer to infirmity.

Ultimately, however, the most peculiar aspect of any birthday party is this: what you are really celebrating is the occasion of extraordinary pain you put your mother through on your original day of birth. Is this really something to celebrate?

That's Entertainment?

ARTS AND ENTERTAINMENT

*"No one ever went broke underestimating the
taste of the American public."*

H.L. Mencken

The only problem with "going out" is that you're going to have to associate with other people. This is, implicitly, bad news. The truth is that as soon as you step outside your door you'll run into hordes of pushy, irksome, disagreeable jerks. In other words, people not unlike yourself. What's more, at any event that's worth attending, you're going to run into a lot of them. While people at different events are markedly different–a ballet crowd, for instance, will be different than a circus crowd and a circus crowd will be different from the crowd at a demolition derby–underneath they're all human beings and thus pretty much guaranteed to get on your nerves. They will sit in front of you with umbrellas up. They'll cut in front of you in refreshment lines. They'll step on your toes coming from and going to their seats. Consequently, you'll end up wishing you'd stayed home and watched television. It may not be good, but at least it's easy.

THE MOVIES

Movies are mostly attended by adolescents. This is largely because adolescents will do almost anything to get out of the house and that includes watching Brooke Shields act. Another reason for this is that adolescents are, by definition, callow and thus can still be amused by the trite, offal Hollywood typically heaves our way.

At any rate unless you go to foreign or "art" films the fact is that you can pretty much count on being surrounded by teenagers. The implications of this are not altogether delightful. This means, for instance, there will be someone seated behind you slurping a soda pop from a container the size of the average garbage can, which may be tipped over to slide icily down the back of your neck or sluice stickily over your shoes. It means that there will be a lot of bobbing, weaving heads in front of you covered with enormous quantities of opaque and extraordinarily vertical hair. It means that you will be surrounded by people who, when not loudly revealing the movie's plot or discussing a friend's new love interest, will be noisily chomping on popcorn from a container the size of a small silo. It means that if you ever work up the nerve to complain about not being able to see or having a soda pop tipped down your neck, you will find yourself in a rude discussion with a threatening juvenile who is at his hormonal and physical peak and probably on steroids besides. Ultimately, it also means that if you get up to run away, you will find your shoes glued to the floor by a tacky pastiche of discarded gum, spilled soda pop and errant hairspray; this is the closest a human can come to getting caught on fly paper.

THE THEATER

In serious, dramatic plays I've often witnessed the most painful and profound expression of human suffering imaginable. This is the sad spectacle of someone who desperately wants to go to sleep but is fighting to stay awake. I've watched as eyelids gratefully slid shut and chins slowly drooped towards chests then, just as the poor souls in question were about to drift blissfully off to sleep, the horrid realization that they'd paid sixty dollars per ticket jolted them awake with the stunning impact of an Ibsen climax. Grimly, chins were lifted from chests. Ruefully, eyelids struggled open. Regretfully, the show went on. This was, in my opinion, true tragedy.

You see, one of the indisputable universal truths implicit in the works of all our great dramatists is that it's not always easy to stay awake during their productions. I mean, let's face it, unless you've read the condensed versions, you won't have the foggiest idea as to what Shakespeare's tragedies are about until they get to the part where everybody kills everybody else and, by that time, they're just about over. As for Shakespeare's comedies, well, four hundred years ago they might have been funny, but then again, so was Henny Youngman. And why, oh why, have playwrights like Clifford Odets concluded that the public wants to go to a play and watch people who are unhappy and bored and argue all the time? Honestly, if that's what we'd wanted, we could have just stayed home.

Of course, not all plays are dull and plodding. Some are lively and interesting. These are the kind of plays you can't get tickets for. If you can, rest assured, your seats will be far enough away from the stage so that you will seem to be looking at a puppet show. "Who are those people down there?" you will ask yourself "And what are they saying?" For this you paid sixty dollars!? And let's not forget to add in ten dollars for parking, three dollars to check your coat, three dollars for a cup of coffee to help you stay awake after intermission, and the cost of getting get mugged on the way home.

Finally, of course, there are Broadway musicals. Despite the fact that these are typically written to attract and to amuse people from the suburbs of New Jersey and will thus be less likely to engage your intellect than the average menu, you can nonetheless, feel pretty confident that you will never feel drowsy during one of these performances. That's simply because these shows typically feature at least one performer with a voice similar to that of the late Ethel Merman's. Sleep will be out of the question. Ear damage will not.

THE DANCE

There are a few things we can all learn from "The Dance." First, is that any form of entertainment starting with "The" is likely to take itself far too seriously and should probably be avoided. When you go to a performance of "The Dance," just as when you go to "The Theater," you're likely to find yourself appreciating it much more than enjoying it, and before long you'll have trouble staying awake.

The other thing we learn from "The Dance" is what a truly horrible and ugly thing the human body is. While there are certain bodies in the realm of nature worth watching, they're certainly not human. Even at it's best the human body is likely to look like an underfed ape and, in either case, Adam and Eve were right to be ashamed. Unfortunately, this undermines the whole point of going to see "The Ballet," since the indisputable fact is that "The Ballet" doesn't give you much to look at other than human bodies. There's not even a ball or puck involved to occasionally distract you, and generally the costumes are skimpy to the point of non-existence.

Speaking of skimpy, even when the costumes aren't, the plots are. In classical ballet, you generally get to watch while a bunch of woman do a not very convincing job of pretending to be swans. But why would you want to watch anyway? Seriously, what kind of person does it take to sit and stare at some poor, young woman walking on her toes while her feet bleed? You would like to think this peculiar fascination for deformed female feet had gone out of fashion with the elimination of the passion for the bound "lotus foot" among Chinese. But no. Sadly, we still have our devotees of "The Dance" who, for sheer sadism, must rank right up there with the aficionados of pitbull fighting.

On the other hand, there's always modern dance. Here you don't have to watch women pretending to be swans. What you have to watch are people who often seem to have difficulty picking themselves up off the floor. They wriggle, writhe and generally squirm around in an effort to express life's angst, pain and boredom. Of course it would be hard to deny that somebody knocking across a hardwood floor on her knees would have a profound understanding of pain and probably angst, but I would argue that boredom would be more keenly felt by someone forced to sit on a folding chair in a hot gymnasium and witness this spectacle.

Last, there is folk ballet! Hey! Hey! People clapping their hands! Hey! Hey! Women in bandanas. Hey! Hey! Guys in shirts with big, puffy sleeves. Hey! Hey! Clapping! Skipping! Jumping! Hey! Hey! Hey! And that's just the first dance! Hey! Hey! Hey! For the second dance you'll see exactly the same thing! Hey! Hey! Same with the third. Hey! Hey! Hey! Same for every other dance for the rest of the evening including the encore. Hey! Hey! Hey! HEEEEEEEYYYYY!!!

The truly sad thing is that in order to bring all these advanced forms of boring the public to a state of perfection, a young dancer must practice hours a day for years and years and still never get to perform for anyone other than close friends and kind relatives. Honestly, can't they think of some better way of wasting their childhoods?

ART MUSEUMS

Most people are simply not art lovers. They simply don't see the point of covering a wall with pictures of people they aren't related to and don't even know. Thus there's no need to explain to them why wandering through an art museum is a slow, painful process akin to Christmas shopping or taking a twenty-mile hike in shoes that are too tight. Once in an art museum, they will carp and complain incessantly. "My three-year-old could draw this!" they will groan. "When can we go home?" they will grumble. In short, if forced to go to an art museum, they will do everything they can to make sure that anyone within earshot enjoys the experience as little as they do.

Even if you're an art aficionado, however, you may not enjoy going to an art museum. First, because if there's a great exhibit that you really want to see, it will probably be sold out and you won't be able to get in. Even if you do get in, you still won't be able to see much. Most of the time there will simply be too many people standing in front of you. Thus, instead of looking at work by Matisse, Van Gogh or Gauguin, what you'll mostly see is bald guys' glistening heads from the rear, tall people's hairy ears from below, old ladies' new, blue hairdos and the frizzy, flying froth of art students' untamed manes. No matter how you look at them, these things are rarely beautiful and hardly ever art.

There are, on the other hand, some exhibits you can easily get into see without ordering tickets months in advance or standing in line forever. These are exhibits like the Roman funerary monument collection and the Egyptian wing. Just remember, however, there's a reason this stuff doesn't draw a crowd. No one wants to look at it.

MUSIC

A ha," you're probably saying to yourself, "now what could possibly be wrong with music? What kind of preposterous crank could possibly find anything bad to say about music?" Well, before you go calling me a preposterous crank, I'd just like to say three words that I think will prove my case. These words are "Japanese" and "stringed instruments." A few other words I might add are "opera," "free-form jazz," "native American chants" and, of course, "Arnold Schoenberg." By the way, on his deathbed, Arnold Schoenberg said that he regretted every note he'd ever written. So does everyone else.

Admittedly, however, it would be churlish to contend that music is not often enjoyable. It is, as long as you stay home and listen to music by yourself. It's when other people enter the picture that the experience will begin to grate on you. At a Pete Seeger concert, for instance, there's the performer by himself. At a Grateful Dead concert, for instance, there's the humiliating possibility that somebody you know might actually see you there. At many rock or rap concerts, there's the audience, most of which would not have the slightest compunction about breaking the aerial off your car and whipping you with it while demanding your wallet. Finally, at a performance of classical music–the only occasion that's more smug and sanctimonious than an Episcopal church sevice–there's always the outright danger of being bored to death. Besides, if music is the food of love, what's for dessert?

DINING OUT

"Man seldom thinks with more earnestness of anything than he does of his dinner."

Samuel Johnson

Frequently we hear of British men, often quite powerful ones, who are willing to pay large sums of money in order to be treated with scorn and contempt, and to pursue their shameful desires in hidden bordellos. These men are called masochists. In the U.S. on the other hand, people who have a taste for humiliation and are willing to pay exorbitant sums to satisfy their cravings may do so on virtually any street in the country. These people are called restaurant goers.

When one goes to a restaurant, you see, one expects to be mortified. The captain, if there is a captain, will make you wait for a seat until you either slip him an unconscionable bribe or it's his pleasure to lead you to someplace that's the dining equivalent of Kamchatka. Once you're seated, the waiter or waitress, as the title implies, will make you wait and wait and wait. First, they'll make you wait until they're good and ready to take your order. Then they'll make you wait for them to bring your meal. (Commonly this is when the hot food's cold, the cold's food's hot and when the ice in a drink has melted. This is how they know it's time for you to be served.) Why is it, you might wonder, that many waiters and waitresses act as though they are celebrities and you are someone who is, irritatingly, asking for an autograph? The answer is that many waiters and waitresses don't truly consider themselves waiters and waitresses but rather actors, painters, sculptors, dancers and what have you. In short, they fully expect someday to be celebrities who will have every right in the world to treat some you with disdain and contempt. So why wait?

However, the real problem in restaurants is not really the general surliness of the servitors. The real problem is the food. I don't just mean such negligible difficulties as the taste either; you might end up eating shrimp that's reminiscent of old ballet slippers, wine that evokes nails in brine and the grey, gritty gristle of the omnipresent hamburger pattie. After all, this kind of putrid food is something we've come to expect. What I'm talking about is the fact that at at every single restaurant in the country a certain number of rat hairs, rodent droppings, spores, larvae and bug parts are legally permissible in everything you eat. This means every time you munch into that taco burger, chomp down on that three-bean salad or dig into that fresh mince pie, you're probably chewing something that wasn't listed on the menu, such as a mite or a meal worm. Appetizing, huh? What's more, this revolting likelihood doesn't even take into consideration the stuff that goes into the food at every restaurant in the world, that's legally impermissible, such as the human effluvia secreted onto it by those involved in its preparation. Yeah, that's right. I'm talking about the spittle spritzed onto your salad by a resentful busboy who will never make more than the minimum wage, the furtive booger flicked at your burger by an alcoholic dishwasher, and the small crescent of ear wax carefully worked into the crust of your cheese fondu by a disgruntled sous-chef. And what about those lumps in your tapioca pudding? Do you really think that they all belong there? Bon appetit.

PARTIES

Although parties take many shapes and forms–from cocktail and dinner parties to theatrical opening parties–there are fundamentally only two kinds. In the most typical instance, the party will be attended by the same, old boring people you've known since the world began. You will talk about all the same, old boring stuff you've always talked about, and spend the evening wondering when you can politely announce your departure and leave.

In rarer instances, the host or hostess will go to great pains in order to bring together a disparate and interesting group of "new people." In this case, two things can happen. One, the new people will be just as dull and boring as the old people. They will tell you how many children they have, what they do for a living, and generally make you wish you had a hearing aid so that you could turn it off. Without much effort, they can casually ruin an evening. On the other hand, the "new people" may be great raconteurs who lead fascinating lives and are only too happy to spend the evening telling you all about themselves. In short, these people will make you feel worthless and dull, and are capable of not just casually ruining an evening but possibly your entire life. I mean, really, what do you say to someone who's just returned from Zambia and discovered a potential clue to a cure for cancer? "Yeah, well I just cut the lawn"?

There are, of course, many pluses and minuses to all sorts of parties. At a cocktail party, for instance, the upside is that, in addition to getting all you want to drink for free, you can usually escape from any conversation merely by indicating that you're thirsty. The downside, however, is that you'll probably have to eat something damp on a stale cracker. Conversely, at a dinner party, while the food is usually as good as what you get in a mediocre restaurant, you can usually get all you want for free by occasionally grinning at the host. The downside is the claustrophobic terror of knowing that, once you're seated next to someone who bores you to death, there's no escape until after the sorbet is served. You'll simply have to sit there and listen to him, until it's time to politely announce your departure and leave. Dinner parties, of course, also present us with one of the great, unsolvable conundrums of our culture: how to get through an occasion during which you're expected to eat and talk at the same time, without showing everyone you're talking to what you're chewing on. Naturally, your mother probably told you that you weren't supposed to do this, but she never told you exactly how, did she? The only good part of this is that if you do eat and talk at the same time, you may get invited to a lot less dinner parties.

When all is said and done, however, the main reason to attend any kind of party is not the free food or the free drink but simply that if you don't, you will inevitably become a topic of conversation yourself. You and all your less applaudable habits will be dished up, cut apart, mulled over, chewed to pieces and devoured with at least as much relish as the food. So, maybe you'd better go.

THE TUBE

"Television is a vast wasteland."

Newton Minnow

If there's anything more American than apple pie, it's watching television. Clearly it's our first love. However, this is clearly not because we love television shows so much. After all, what are we likely to see? A sitcom that will be precisely like several hundred others we've already seen, with a laugh track to remind us when the show's funny in case we forgot? Or perhaps a cops and robbers show in which the good guys always win? So why do we spend hour after slack-jawed hour, night after mind-numbing night, bathing in that ghoulish, blue glow?

As near as I can figure out, there are two main reasons. One is that watching TV is as close as we can get to actually doing nothing and still be considered alive. In short, it's our national mania for lassitude that permits us to plunk our big bottoms down on our plump, pillowed couches and sit there all night, night after night, with only the few brief punctuations necessary for alimentary elimination or the replenishment of an empty popcorn bowl.

But probably the more compelling reason we love TV is that it allows us to ignore each other with complete and imperturbable impunity. You see, the magic of television isn't that it brings the world into your living room, but rather that it keeps it out. Magically, it reduces human beings from the loud, annoying gorilla-like creatures they are in person to little, itty-bitty pictures you can turn off with the flick of a switch. Thus, face-to-face confrontations with the billions of foul-breathed simians who are our irksome brethren on this planet become virtually unnecessary. Similarly, TV helps us to ignore our families. When all heads are turned in the same direction and all eyes are focused on the one-eyed monster, we can avoid or eliminate eye contact. With the volume up and constant admonitions of "Shut up, I wanna hear!" we do away with the possibility of conversation. Thus, wrapped in this cocoon of video rapture, we become impervious, imperturbable and godlike. No wonder we love it. Besides, what else are you going to do? Read?

CARTOONS

We protect out children from the violence they would otherwise be exposed to on TV, by letting them watch cartoons. What do they see? Wile E. Coyote getting ground into hamburger; Elmer Fudd raging like some dwarfish psychopath, indiscriminately firing his shootgun into a crowd. They see Ninja Turtles eviscerating opponents with exotic, oriental implements of destruction; in short, animals, robots and distorted forms of humanity constantly engaged in cruel and colorful acts of vicious mutual destruction. Now just where do you suppose kids get the idea violence is any way to solve a problem?

SITCOMS

Every once in a while there's a good sitcom. Of course, every once in a while someone gets swallowed by a whale and lives, too. Typically, however, any sitcom we see is exactly like one we've seen several hundred times before: Dad's sort of a dork and the kids are impish, while Mom's in charge. Hardee har.

DRAMAS, SOAP OPERAS,
COPS AND ROBBERS SHOWS

You can accurately predict the conclusion of nine out of ten TV dramas well in advance of actually turning on the tube. The good guys will win, the bad guys will be shot several dozen times. I hope you don't stay awake nights wondering how these things are going to turn out.

PBS

Most of these shows star bugs, birds or big mouths from Boston. So how come people don't want to watch?

AFTERWORD: I'D LIKE TO SAY JUST FUN MORE THING

Can you recall how nice it is to wake up some mornings, look out the window and notice that it's raining? Especially Saturday mornings, when you invariably have a vast agenda of unavoidable amusement laid out before you? You know, you've probably planned golf, going to the beach, a cookout with friends and family. Do you remember how wonderful it feels when you see that heavenly liquid streaming down in unabating sheets, and breathing a sigh of relief you can simply crawl back into bed?

Well, I say, let's pretend that every day's a rainy day. After all, if you don't feel like going to the beach, for God's sake, don't go. I don't care if the sun's bright, and the sky's blue. And if you don't feel like playing golf, just say "no." Objectively considered, it's a miserable enough activity anyway; and if you don't feel like playing, it's doubly so. I, for one, think a full day spent in bed, picking your toes and reading a book is at least as enjoyable as one spent hitting a white ball at a bunch of grass–and a whole lot less expensive.

The trouble is, in this culture, people just don't want to let you alone. In fact, by the end of today or, certainly, this weekend, you just know some nincompoop will be trying to force you to do something in the name of fun that you don't want to do at all. It could be anything from playing a new "fun" game to trying a new "fun" food to using a new "fun" drug to assuming a new "fun" sexual position. Before you know it, you'll be having a rotten time and wish you were home in bed, picking your toes and reading a book.

At any rate now that you've read this book, I hope you'll be able to recognize the many forms of fun for what they are; needless overstimulations of the central nervous system that are usually harmful to your health or a pointless, waste of time. And the next time someone says "Awwww, come on, it'll be fun," I trust you'll have the strength of character to turn to that person and, swelling with righteous indignation, simply reply, "I HATE FUN!"

Somewhat sincerely,

Mifflin Lowe